The GOD who answers by FIRE

By Margaret Cleator

STL Books
PO Box 48, Bromley, Kent, England
PO Box 28, Waynesboro, Georgia, USA

Copyright © 1966 BMMF International
Second edition 1976
Revised edition 1986

STL Books are published by Send The Light (Operation Mobilisation), PO Box 48, Bromley, Kent, England.

British Library Cataloguing in Publication Data

Cleator, Margaret
    The God who answers by fire.—Rev.ed.
    1. Christianity—India   2. India—Church history
    I. Title
    275.4   BR1155

ISBN 1 85078 005 6

Typesetting and page make-up by Creative Editors & Writers Ltd., Hampermill Cottage, Watford WD1 4PL.
Covers printed by Penderel Press Ltd, Croydon, Surrey.
Made and printed in Great Britain by Hunt Barnard Printing Ltd, Aylesbury, Bucks.

CONTENTS

	Characters	6
1	Sorrow Hits the Family	7
2	Stricken by Grief	12
3	Search for Truth	17
4	The Road to Nagpur	20
5	Temple of the Nag	26
6	Coconut Offerings	31
7	Temples of a Thousand Gods	35
8	Swami Narayan	46
9	Jungle Ablaze	50
10	The Enlightened One	54
11	Holy Fire	69
12	Death to the Old Arjun	71
13	Talegaon—and a Shock	78
14	Arjun Rejected	82
15	A Fool for God	88
16	A New Man	92
17	Sakharam Counts the Cost	97
18	Arjun's Opportunity	105
19	Atmaram Decides	113
20	Arjun to the Rescue!	117
21	Recovery	123
22	Reconciliation	128
23	A Day of Victory	132
24	New Beginnings	138
	Glossary	143

CHARACTERS

Arjun Bhaskar: the central character, a young student

Vishram: Arjun's father

Drupadibai: Arjun's mother

Balkrishna: Arjun's younger brother

Ragunath: Arjun's cousin

Baliram: a lorry driver

Santosh: a farmer

Krupabai: Santosh's wife

Sakharam: Santosh's employer, a wealthy farmer

Vijay: Sakharam's youngest son

Gopichand: wealthy land-owner and money-lender

Atmaram: Gopichand's eldest son

Ganpat: one of Gopichand's younger sons

The Patil: village headman

Note

The incidents in this story are taken from the author's personal experience. The characters are all real people who lived in some town or village of Maharashtra when this book was written, although some are placed here in different situations.

1
Sorrow Hits the Family

The rickety old bus shuddered to a standstill beside a small signboard on which was written *Talegaon 2 miles*. The cloud of dust which had been following the bus now overtook it and smothered its occupants through the open windows. A young man of about twenty-three years self-consciously clambered down on to the dusty road. He wore a clean white suit and brand new black shoes, and carried a new zip hold-all. The other passengers, dressed in their village *pagdis* and *dhotis*, stared at him as he made his way along the cart track that led to Talegaon.

'That's Vishram's boy,' said one.

'Been to college,' said another, spitting his disapproval out of the window.

The conversation was lost in the roar of the engine as the bus laboured to get up speed.

Arjun looked ruefully down at his polished shoes, which were rapidly becoming a dull grey in the thick dust of the track. 'I shall have to wipe them before I get to the village,' he thought. He took a new white handkerchief out of his coat pocket and dusted his suit, and flicked it across the hold-all. Then, having put a comb through his hair, he felt more pleased with himself and the world in general. All he needed now was a transistor radio under his arm, blaring out the latest cinema songs, then he really would be 'with it'! But the price was beyond the pockets of a poor village student who had struggled through college on a scholarship, and had lived on the hard-earned savings of his parents and the charity of his uncle in the city of Nagpur. However, he *had* passed his exam—he was actually a B.A.! He had been prepared to live with B.A. (fail) after his name, but the gods had favoured him and now he was a *pakka* B.A. (pass). He had a coconut in his bag which he was going to offer at the shrine of Ganpati, the elephant god, who had brought him such good luck. He was going to do this for his parents' sake. He was grateful to them for spending so much on his education, and he knew they would expect him to acknowledge some kind of supernatural influence in his life; but as for himself, he was not sure about God. Life in college had changed his whole outlook. The dependent, superstitious attitude of his village relatives was quite out of keeping with the independent, sophisticated city life to which he had grown accustomed— a life in which one determined one's own destiny through education, scientific knowledge and modern culture. If there was a God, he certainly seemed superfluous for the educated person. His father was illiterate, so it was all right for him to offer sacrifices to his gods to ensure a good harvest so that the excess money could go towards his son's education.

Arjun did not allow himself to think of the

thousands of B.A. graduates who were without jobs. Many of them were too proud to do manual work. Having been trained as white-collar workers, they considered it beneath their dignity to work with their hands. Others simply could not get work at all in the situation caused by the exploding population. He was confident that he would be an exception and would find a good job in a city, and earn plenty of money to be able to send his younger brother to college and perhaps send his little sister to high school so that she could be married to an educated husband. He was very fond of his little sister, Tara, who was six years old. He had bought some material for a dress for her, and some pretty bangles. In his bag he also had a sari for his mother, a *dhoti* and shirt for his father, and material for a shirt and pants for his young brother, Balkrishna, who was twelve. Arjun had been fortunate in getting a temporary job in an office while awaiting the exam results, and he had tasted the proud thrill of independence when he received his first wages for a month's work ... 'Education—it is *everything*!' he mused.

His day dreams were interrupted by a shout from the field which he was passing.

'*Ka, ho*! Have you come?' It was his uncle who was laboriously walking behind the plough as the bullocks plodded over the rock-like earth. 'How did it go?'

'I have passed,' Arjun shouted back proudly. 'I am a B.A.'

'*Shabash*! [Well done!]' replied his uncle. 'Your father and mother are waiting for you. Tara is ill.'

A cloud darkened Arjun's bright horizon. What was wrong? They had not let him know. Surely they would have sent a telegram if it was serious? He hastened his steps and forgot all about wiping his shoes when he came to the village. The sun was about to set when he passed the familiar sight of the well and the idol shrine. The women and girls who were drawing water watched in curiosity, murmuring to each other, 'Vishram's boy.' 'He's been to college.' 'He's educated—look at his clothes!'

'What price his education?' asked an older woman, hoisting her brass vessel on to her head. 'His sister is dying; what then?'

Arjun made his way through the chickens, dogs and goats that roamed the streets, and turned off up a little lane that led to his mud house with its tiled roof and open verandah. He was within a few yards of the house when he heard his mother's voice uplifted in the wail for the dead: '*Meli re, meli re!* [she's dead, she's dead!]'

Other women's voices joined in until the village echoed with the soul-shattering cry of those who are without hope. Arjun's blood froze as he stood paralysed with fear. The neighbours came running to join in the mourning, some to enjoy the scene, others to sympathise with the parents.

'Your sister has died!' shouted a schoolboy cheerfully to Arjun as he ran past him to the house.

Dazed with shock, Arjun pushed his way through the crowd and entered the room. His precious little sister Tara was lying dead on the bed. His mother was leaning over her, calling to her to come back to life and wailing at intervals. His father was squatting on the floor moaning with grief, while his young brother Balkrishna was sobbing in a corner of the room. He had just come in from school and saw his sister breathe her last. It was his first sight of death and he was terribly afraid.

Arjun dropped his new zip bag on the ground and gazed hopelessly at the body. What a home-coming! What a crashing of all his hopes and dreams! What did his education amount to if it could not save life and prevent death and destruction in this world?

His mother looked up and saw him. With renewed wails she threw herself into his arms and they wept together.

2

Stricken by Grief

The village folk had gone to bed. Arjun sat up that
night with his mother and father silently sipping
tea, which was all they could stomach after the funeral ceremony. Wood was scarce, and Tara was
only a girl, so a funeral pyre was not necessary. Her
body had been wrapped in a red cloth and lowered
into a rough grave down by the dry river bed. There
were no flowers, few mourners, and not even a
drum to beat out the heart-breaking rhythm of the
march to the grave. The clods of earth seemed so
very hard and heavy as they thudded down on to
her delicate body while the grave was filled in.
Arjun wanted to cry out in pain for her; it seemed
so wrong to leave her there under that weight of
earth, lonely, deserted. He had looked at his
mother, wondering how she could take it.
Drupadibai was moaning quietly in dejection and
resignation now that the first emotions had died
down. She had seen three other children buried
before this during her married life; it was but the
fate of many women of India. But the gods had
spared her remaining two sons. That, at least, gave
her hope that she was not altogether accursed. She
sat now hunched up by the wall of the room, her

head bowed on her folded arms.

Balkrishna was asleep on the bed where only a few hours before the corpse of Tara had lain. Sorrow and weariness had brought a merciful oblivion to the young boy. He would soon accept her absence in the daily adventure of youth, and he had playmates of his own age at school and in the village.

Vishram put the cup and saucer down. Coming out of his reverie he turned to Arjun.

'So, how did you get on?' he asked.

'I passed,' said Arjun in a toneless voice. Gone was the pride, the satisfaction and anticipation that he had had a few hours before. It did not seem to matter now.

'Good!' said his father more cheerfully than he felt. 'Now you will be able to get a good job.'

Arjun did not answer. Three questions were violently revolving in his mind, insistently crying out for an answer. He knew he had to find that answer...

Where had Tara gone? He could not accept the materialistic outlook of his fellow students who claimed that 'when you are dead you are done for—there is nothing more'. His parents' beliefs of reincarnation into higher or lower forms of life did not hold any comfort. Where was she now? What was on the other side of death?

Why had she been taken? Being the oldest son of the family he had been present when the other three children had died; but they were all babies—his own brothers and sisters, yes, but too young really to concern him. But Tara was a sweet child;

gay, loving and always so pleased to see him. She
never let him out of her sight while he was at home.
Tara was his special joy. Why had she been
taken?—So suddenly too. She had been playing
quite happily the previous day; then in the afternoon she complained of a headache, and all night
she was tossing in a fever. They had called the
bhagat but he could do nothing, and by that afternoon her life was slipping away. Some vicious spirit
must have got into her. How? Why? O God, why?

The third question which automatically followed
these other two was, what was he to do now? He
knew he could not settle down into a job even if he
was lucky enough to get one. This aching void in his
heart would never be satisfied until he had found
the answer to these questions—in reality, until he
had found God.

'How does one become a sadhu?' he asked suddenly.

'A sadhu?' replied his father in astonishment.
'Why a sadhu?'

'I must find God. I must find the answer to life—
to death—I don't know. But I must find the answer.'

'But my son, you are educated,' Vishram pro-
tested. 'Your mother and I have worked hard to
send you to college. You must find a good job with
a high salary so that Balkrishna can go to college
too, and our family debts can be paid, and—and we
can buy better fields and build a bigger house.'

'What good will that do if one of us gets snatched
away like Tara?' asked Arjun gloomily.

'But you can't throw away all your learning and
the money we've spent on you,' Vishram said

anxiously.

'It won't be throwing away the learning if I study the *Bhagwat Gitas* and *Upanishads* more closely, and delve into all the sacred books of the *mahants* and *rishis*.'

'But what profit will that bring you?' persisted his father. 'You receive no salary for that—and where will be all our labour for you?'

'I've never seen a lean sadhu yet!' replied Arjun sarcastically. 'Those who seem to know what they are talking about receive masses of money from their worshippers and do very well.'

His father sat dumb. He knew he should have been proud that a son of his should want to join in the search for Truth and be associated with the priestly ranks of the wise ones of Hinduism, but this was cutting right across his hopes and aspirations for the future—a future which was limited to this world only, where money and material benefits were all that mattered.

'You're tired,' murmured Vishram after a pause. 'Get some sleep and you will feel better in the morning.'

Drupadibai was already asleep. The two men lay down on the verandah in the airless night. But Arjun could not sleep. He was already making his plans. 'People go on pilgrimages when they are searching for God,' he thought. 'I will go to the most famous places first and talk to the *mahants* in each place. By then I should know what I should do.' Then he thought of the coconut he had brought in his bag for the god Ganpati. 'I will offer that in the morning. Maybe he will bless my journey—if he is real.' Then he thought with a pang of the gifts he had brought for Tara. 'I should have buried them with her; she may need them in her next life—but how can one know?'

He thought of what the *Bhagwat Gita* had to say about death: 'The sorrow for the bodily death of friends and kindred is a grief to which wisdom and the true knowledge of life lend no sanction. The enlightened man does not mourn either for the living or the dead, for he knows that suffering and death are merely incidents in the history of the soul. The soul, not the body, is the reality. Human life and death, repeated through the aeons in the great cycles of the world, are only a long progress by which the human being prepares himself for Immortality. Whoever is subject to grief and sorrow, a slave to the sensations and emotions, occupied by the touches of things transient, cannot become fit for Immortality.'

'That may be,' Arjun thought. 'But how can one overcome and be immune to grief for a loved one? If I knew where she had gone, it might be more bearable.'

His thoughts ran on until he fell into an uneasy sleep. He dreamed that he was travelling along an endless dark road, calling out, 'Tara, where are you?' Then, even in his dreams he was conscious that something inside him seemed to break, somehow his desire for Tara was superseded by his desire for God. He heard himself cry out in anguish, 'O God! Where are you? Where are you?'

3
Search for Truth

A few days later Arjun was walking along the main road to Nagpur. He was clothed in a saffron-coloured robe as the Hindu sadhus wear, and wore no shoes on his feet. He was allowing his hair to grow long and his bristly chin showed signs of a new beard. He carried a staff in his hand, and on his back was a blanket, water bottle and cooking pot—all that he felt a sadhu should need who was searching for eternal verities rather than the comforts of this world. He wore no paint or ashes on his forehead or body to show whose devotee he was, for he did not know which god could give him the answers to his questions. He wore no sacred beads or charms for he did not know how to use them or if any had the power that was claimed for them. He would wait and see. He wanted the Truth.

The days at home had been agony to his soul. He had had to harden his heart to his mother's tears, his father's grief-stricken protests, and the advice and warning of his friends and relatives when they heard of this mad idea to throw over everything in search of God. The *ideal* was all right. They all agreed it was a very high aim and purpose, but who in his right mind would throw over a good education and prospects of security and advancement in life—just for God? It was all very well, but...

Arjun's mind had been made up on the morning he offered the coconut at Ganpati's shrine. The sensual shape of the idol with its pot-belly, and shrewd self-satisfied smirk on its elephant face, which he had taken for granted all these years, suddenly appeared to him revolting and disgusting and he resented the giving of even a coconut to this crude carving in dead stone. Why? He was surprised at himself as he walked seven times round the shrine repeating prayers he had learned from childhood, feeling more and more contempt for what he was doing, yet knowing no other way of getting into touch with the Unseen.

'I *must* find the Truth,' he had said to himself as he descended the steps from the shrine, and from that day nothing would deter him.

Now he was on his way to Varanasi, the sacred city of Hinduism, where he was sure he would find the Truth. He would stop at every shrine and temple on the way, and enquire of the resident priest as much as he could tell him. He would join in every *mela* and festival to meet the holy men who came to such places and learn from them; then surely by the time he reached Varanasi he would be prepared to *know*.

He had no money with him, and he would not beg. When he stepped on to the main road from the cart track that led from his village, he had prayed, 'O God, if there is a God, if you are real, prosper me in my journey, lead me, let me find you; and show me that you want me to know you by supplying my needs along the way.'

He went on. He was certain he was doing the right thing, and the pang of leaving his parents in this way was overruled by the anticipation he felt as he started off on this precious quest. He had risen early and left before his parents were awake. He did not want a scene and he had told them he was leaving in the morning, so they would know he had started. When he had found the Truth, he would come back to tell them and his whole village what he had found and bring them into the Light also.

4

The Road to Nagpur

It was terribly hot. June was drawing to a close, and though a few thunder showers had fallen the real monsoon seemed as far away as ever and the atmosphere was stifling. Arjun was pouring with sweat, and his water-bottle was nearly empty. There was little traffic on the road and he still had sixty miles to go before he reached Nagpur. He would pass through a few villages on the way, but none was in sight just then and it was nearly midday. He was about to stop and rest under a tree when he heard the sound of a lorry coming behind him. As it came into view he raised his hand hopefully. The lorry drew up by the side of the road and the driver put his head out of the window.

'Going to Nagpur?' asked Arjun.

'Yes,' said the driver, looking him up and down with interest. 'You're not the usual kind of sadhu, are you?'

Arjun smiled and shook his head. 'I don't quite know what I am, but I want to get to Nagpur.'

'Sure! Jump in,' he said casually.

Baliram was a good-natured fellow, and was used to picking up all kinds of travellers along the road. Arjun clambered up into the driver's cab and they started off.

'I'm stopping soon for a snack. It's too hot to travel at this time of day. Have you had a meal?'

'No,' said Arjun. He had been too thirsty to feel hungry, but now he was beginning to feel really empty.

'Then you can get something at Khondali. They have a good tea stall there.'

Arjun was silent. He did not want to tell him he had no money, and he did not want to appear as if he were dropping hints.

'Are you on pilgrimage?' asked Baliram, glad to have someone to talk to.

'Yes,' said Arjun shyly. He was not used to his new role of sadhu, and he wondered what the reaction of this down-to-earth young man might be.

'How far are you going?'

'To Varanasi.'

'They all go there. Wonder what they find? What are you hoping to find?'

'I want to find God,' said Arjun, waiting for a sneer or a mocking laugh. But the driver took it all in his stride.

'Not many go for that,' he said thoughtfully. 'They want peace, or satisfaction, or good luck in marriage or business, or the promise of a better incarnation. But there aren't many who are looking for God himself.'

'Do you think I'll find him in Varanasi?' asked Arjun, his heart warming to this young man who seemed so matter-of-fact and practical.

Baliram clicked his tongue in the negative. 'I doubt it. They come back from these places like

Varanasi and Pandharpur, and from all the *melas* tired, fed up and disillusioned. They've spent all their money and got nothing in return. If I were you, I wouldn't waste my time or my money. After all, no one believes in God nowadays. It's all right for the old folk who are illiterate and don't know any better, but in this age of machines and atomic energy and space travel, well—God's out of place, if you know what I mean. We have our national gods which are rather like a national emblem, and I like to see the picturesque temples, and some of the customs are nice to keep up, but as for spending your life looking for something that does not exist, well, as I say, it's a waste of time.'

He spoke without any antagonism, just giving plain commonsense advice which made Arjun feel that perhaps after all he was wasting his time. But then...

'Have you ever lost anyone you love very much?' he asked.

Baliram's eyes misted over and he had to clear his throat before he answered.

'I know there are times when one wished one knew,' he said huskily. 'But look at Communism. They have an answer for everything. They concentrate on making this world a better place to live in so there will be no poverty, no high castes exploiting the low castes, and work for everyone, so that no one is wasting time or money finding out about God, but everyone is getting on with the job and building up a happy society in absolute equality. Look at Russia with those lovely factories and houses. Everyone has plenty and is happy—and they got rid of the idea of God a long time ago.'

Arjun had read the glossy magazines that come from Russia by the million, full of Communist propaganda, but he had also heard of the other side of Communism with its persecutions and slave labour and blood purges—and he wondered.

'China is also Communist,' he said.

'China—now China...'

Arjun wondered what words of wisdom were going to come about India's enemy, when they approached the village of Khondali.

'Ah, here's our tea stall!' said Baliram, happily forgetting all about China.

They drew up under a tree and alighted, stretching their cramped muscles. Two other lorries were also standing in the shade of the trees. Their drivers were sitting on benches outside the tea stall, smoking and drinking tea.

'Ram, Ram!' they greeted Baliram. 'Who have you got with you this time?' they asked, looking curiously at Arjun.

'He's a real sadhu, one who really wants to find God,' said Baliram, introducing Arjun to his friends as they sat down.

'Two teas and a plate of those nice *bhajis*,' called Baliram to the man inside.

'I'll just have water,' Arjun said hastily. 'I need to fill my water-bottle.'

He went to the water tub and filled his bottle. Baliram had understood the situation.

'You are my guest,' he said when Arjun returned. 'I would like to treat you to this.'

'That is very kind of you,' said Arjun. He would

have been embarrassed if he had not been so relieved at this sign of favour on his journey—his needs being supplied!

While he tucked into the *bhajis*, Baliram went on explaining to his friends:

'This chap isn't the usual kind of parasite that clutters up our society. He doesn't beg—as you see, he would have just made do with water, and—I say,' he said turning to Arjun, 'where were you educated?'

'Nagpur University,' replied Arjun, feeling a glow of pride in spite of this strange situation.

'There you are!' said Baliram to his friends. 'Given up all that education to find God. That's what I call sacrifice—even though there may be no God at the end of it! It's a high ideal—a—a—' he could not think of the right word and his friends smiled at his enthusiasm.

'All right, why don't you throw up your job and do the same?' asked one, laughing coarsely.

'Not me!' said Baliram quickly, 'I'm not that sort. Anyway, I've got two kids to support,' and he changed the subject.

Within an hour they were on the road again.

'I left my mate sick in Amraoti,' Baliram resumed his philosophising. 'He's a Christian. He says there is a God who came to this world once, and he is going to come again. But he doesn't seem to know much about him, except that he died for our sins or something. And he doesn't agree with Communism. We have great arguments but we've never convinced each other yet.'

'The Christians are a strange mixture. I don't

think they could have the answer,' said Arjun, dismissing them from his mind. He had met a few nominal Christian students at college, but he had seen no difference in them from the others.

'Anyway, Christianity is dope from the West,' Baliram continued, having memorised passages from the colourful magazines. 'Look how the missionaries bribed and exploited the poor people of our country, then told them to be content with their lot because it was God's will for them. This is why India has never advanced all these years. Only now are we beginning to break off the shackles of the West and their religious dope and deceit, and we are able to stand on our own feet.'

Arjun did not reply. He was not sure how true that previous statement was.

They drove into Nagpur.

'Where do you want to get down?' asked Baliram.

'Anywhere will do. I have to take the road to the north.'

'Then you are not far from it here,' said Baliram. 'Keep straight on up this road and you will see sign posts to Jabalpur. That's your first big town. I have to turn off to the left here.'

Arjun thanked him and got down.

As he started off Baliram called after him, 'Let me know if you find God. I should like to know. I'm on this trip every week from Bombay to Nagpur.'

5
Temple of the Nag

It was near sunset. Arjun did not immediately follow the road to the north. He fell in with a few evening worshippers who were going to the temple of the Nag (cobra) from which Nagpur derived its name.

While the worshippers were noisily ringing the bell in the outer porch and walking seven times round the five-headed bronze image of the cobra, muttering their prayers automatically with no expectation of an answer, Arjun slipped into the inner precincts where no one was allowed to go except the priest. The devotees of Shiva were allowed in only once a year at Nag Panchmi, the festival of the cobra.

The inner temple was completely dark except for a glimmer of light coming from the flame of an oil lamp which stood before the golden idol of the Nag. The neck was erect and the hood spread as if the snake was about to strike. In the deep shadows it looked the very symbol of evil. Arjun shuddered.

A priest was standing in front of the idol, clothed in a saffron robe, his head shaved in the manner of the Brahmans with one lock of hair in the centre. His hands were together in prayer. His voice

boomed in a low echo up to the dome of the temple
as he slowly repeated the Sanskrit interpretation of
the ineffable name of God: 'Oummm ... Oummm
... Oummm ...' Each word faded away like the
clang of a deep-toned bell.

Arjun stood watching and listening. His heart
grew colder and colder as he felt the powers of evil
close in around him. He was surrounded by a great
wall of darkness. He wanted to escape but he was
hypnotised by this strange power. He wanted to
speak to the priest and ask questions, but he could
not open his mouth—something seemed to be
clutching at his throat. Then, utterly fascinated by
that gleaming image and overpowered by the
atmosphere, he dropped on his knees and put his
forehead to the ground in obeisance to the god.

The priest's voice boomed on: 'Oummm ...
Oummm ... Oummm...'

Arjun tore himself away. He was pouring with
sweat as he came down the temple steps. It was a
hot sultry evening, but that was not the only reason
for his feeling of exhaustion. He came from the side
street into the main thoroughfare of Nagpur, into
the modern city with its shops, cinemas, cars and
buses, into the twentieth century.

'If that is God,' thought Arjun, wiping his
perspiring face with a corner of his robe, 'then I am
afraid of him. I don't want to know him. It is better
to concentrate on this life only, for as Baliram says,
"God seems out of place in our modern world."
But, supposing he does exist, what then? What terrible punishment will he mete out to those who have
ignored him in this life? Where has Tara gone? Is

she—is she in the grip of an evil power like that?'
The thought was too terrible.

He went on. By the time he reached the outskirts
of the city it was growing dark. He had had nothing
to eat all day except those few *bhajis* at the tea stall,
but after that experience in the temple he had no
appetite. He had planned to sleep under a tree
somewhere along the road, but now he was afraid
to be alone in the dark. He imagined that the evil
power would catch up with him and torment him for
the rest of his life, and surely that is what hell must
be like!

'Sadhuji!' a woman's voice called to him from a
cottage near by. 'Please come here.'

He turned and saw her standing in the doorway
with a brass plate in her hands.

'Please take this,' she said, as he approached.

He saw that it was a good meal of rice and curry
and *chapatis*. Arjun was amazed; another sign of
favour upon his journey in spite of what had just
happened?

'The priest has told me that if I feed every holy
man and give alms to every beggar who passes by,
the gods will give me a child. So please eat,' she
explained.

Arjun took the plate, sat down on the step and
started to eat. At the sight of the food he realised
how hungry he was, and ate with relish. The woman
put a glass of water beside him and watched him.
She was about thirty years of age, and for an Indian
woman to attain that age without the birth of a child
was a terrible disgrace.

'Is your husband here?' asked Arjun when he

had finished.

'No, he—he has gone to make other arrangements.' Tears welled up in her eyes. She covered her face with her sari.

'I understand,' Arjun said sympathetically.

In fact, seeing the situation from this unusual angle, he understood for the first time in his life the miserable plight of a childless wife—the curses from her husband, the taunts and jibes from relatives and neighbours, the humiliation of being treated as a slave by the second wife, and enduring her taunts and sarcasm when her child was born. Then there was the fear of the anger of the gods, and the hopelessness of ever being freed from the endless cycle of transmigration through some sin she had committed in a past incarnation.

'Perhaps,' he thought, 'perhaps Tara has escaped all that. Perhaps she is better off now.'

But even as the feeling of relief came, the remembrance of that atmosphere in the temple came to him and again he feared.

'Is there anywhere I can sleep here?' he asked.

'There is a shed here by the house. You may sleep there,' she said, leading him to a lean-to shed where her husband worked as a carpenter and repairer of cart wheels.

She returned to the house. Arjun spread his blanket on the floor and lay down on his back with his arms above his head. It was still very hot, with not a breath of air. It would not be possible to sleep until the early hours. He would have slept outside, but then he thought the woman's name might be besmeared as her husband was away. It would be better that no one saw him there ...

He thought ironically that if he had been the usual kind of sadhu or *bhagat* he would have offered to sleep with her—then the gods would have given her a child. 'And that would be wrong,' his thoughts roamed on. 'But then, how do I know it is wrong? If God is only evil, as he seemed to be in that temple—how do I know what is good? There must be a good God somewhere. There is Ganesh who protects us from evil spirits, and Skhanda who fights the armies of evil, but are they really God? Who is God? What is he? Or is it just a power, a force that upholds the universe—that pure spiritual essence, impersonal, bodiless, passionless, which diffuses itself everywhere like electricity and radio waves—gods, men, animals, plants and rivers being the manifestation of this essence, as the Brahmans teach? If so, then what do good or evil matter anyway? And if they do not matter, why should people be punished for doing wrong?'

The more he thought, the more Baliram's philosophy seemed to be acceptable. Should he go back? Was it worth going on? But—was not this second favour of a meal, so unexpected, a sign that some power was leading him on? And had not Baliram himself really wanted to know about God? He determined he would go on. Cost what it may, he would search until he found the answer.

6

Coconut Offerings

It was the full moon of the goddess of the Narbada River. Thousands of pilgrims lined the river banks intently watching the worship of the goddess. Men and women stood in the water as far as they dared to go, for the river was in spate, the rains having broken in torrents. The water was a dark muddy brown colour, terrifying in its swiftness, carrying all kinds of debris and the bodies of drowned animals.

The worshippers each had a coconut which they had broken on a stone by the river. Half they gave to the priest who stood waist deep in the water, and half they presented to the idol of the goddess which had been taken out of the temple and placed at the river's edge. The priest chanted a prayer to the goddess while he performed a sensual kind of dance in the water. Then he threw the half coconut into the river while each worshipper paid homage to the idol. The goddess was draped in hundreds of garlands made of sweet smelling flowers which her worshippers had placed there. Incense was burning at the four corners of the red mat on which the idol stood. As each offering was made, men with tomtoms and cymbals beat out a rhythm which accompanies every festival where the idols are worship-

ped. Gifts of money, jewels and food were laid at
her feet.

Arjun mingled with the crowds. He was footsore,
weary and wet. He had only been able to get a lift as
far as Seoni, which left him ninety-one miles to
walk as far as Jabalpur. Lorries and cars had not
stopped for him—probably afraid or unwilling to
pick up this 'parasite that clutters up our society', as
Baliram had remarked. Food had been fairly plen-
tiful each time he had taken shelter from the rain in
some village or hamlet. The people of the house
gladly gave him a meal, considering it a privilege to
feed a holy man. But he received no money. That,
at first, did not worry him until he had gone to see
a *rishi* who practised yoga in some hills to the north
of Seoni.

Arjun remembered that incident. He had saluted
the *yogi* respectfully, placing his hands together in
worship. The *yogi* had looked straight through him
and said nothing. He was sitting in the lotus position, legs crossed with soles turned upward and
resting on the knees. Arjun waited. The *yogi*
neither blinked or moved, nor did he visibly
breathe.

Finally Arjun said, 'Swamiji, I have a question to
ask.'

There was silence for another minute, then the
yogi said in a far-away voice, 'You have brought no
offering?'

Arjun had not thought of it. He had not come to
ask a favour, but a question.

'I have no money,' he said apologetically.

'You come into the presence of God with empty

hands?' the statue asked, still looking through Arjun as if he was not there.

Arjun drew back. Of course he should have known. From his childhood he had been told how the gods demanded offerings and sacrifices. If they did not have what they each specifically wanted the priest would curse the offender and terrible punishment would befall him. Since Arjun had been to college he had seen through all that, and had realised that it was just an excuse for the priests to fill their pockets and their stomachs. But now it dawned on him that unless he offered these people money and gifts he would not get the answer he was seeking.

He said quietly, 'I wanted to ask you if you had found God.'

There was no answer.

Arjun had already decided he would not beg. Many sadhus and *bhagats* would threaten the village people with curses if they did not give anything. The poor people in superstitious fear would give more than they could afford. 'The next time anyone offers me a meal, I will ask for money instead,' Arjun thought. But the next time he was offered food was nearly a day later, and he was so hungry and weak from his long walk that he gladly accepted and did not have the heart to ask for money.

Now he had arrived at the *mela* and had no money to buy a coconut or give a gift to the priest. He stood and watched the worshippers and the priest performing the rituals mechanically, without any sign of reverence or devotion, as a mere ceremony which had to be done in order to get on well in this life and have a better existence later on. It seemed to Arjun that it did not matter if he brought an offering or not. The gifts offered here were nothing more than bribes to the deity to bring them good luck, and to the priest so that he should perform his mediatorial offices for them and keep them in the good books of the deity. 'If he is the kind of God that hides behind all that, he is not worth knowing,' thought Arjun.

Then he prayed, 'God, if you are still leading me—you have given me food all this time—please give me money *if I need it to find you*. If not, if I don't need it, and can find you just as well without, then it doesn't matter.'

He did not receive a single *paisa* during the whole of his journey!

7

Temples of a Thousand Gods

Arjun walked on for another two weeks, stopping
here and there to ask questions of sadhus, *rishis*,
priests and *mahants*, but none could give him a
definite answer. All they could offer him were for-
mulas, offerings which had to be given at certain
times and festivals, *mantras* to say at certain sea-
sons, and always fasts and feasts to be kept, the
Bhagwat Gita and *Upanishads* to study and recite
ad infinitum. Some would not give any advice
because he had no money to offer, others were willing to help and to show off the knowledge they
had, but none could say, 'I have found God.'

Arjun had studied the *Bhagwat Gita* and *Vedanta*
at college, not in detail as a priest would, but he had
a good idea of what it contained, and as far as he
was concerned it did not have the answer. For if, as
the *Bhagwat Gita* claimed, Krishna is One with the
Infinite Self and is concealed in every heart, how
can 'the veil of ignorance which covers the inner
sanctuary' be 'withdrawn to hear the voice of
Krishna, the very voice of God'? The people who
had practised bodily austerities, and spent long
hours in meditation, seemed no nearer the goal

than he. He had read some of the laws of Manu, but they were far too intricate and involved for a man of the world to take seriously. Once again he felt that Baliram's philosophy was the best. But— something drove him on.

At last he reached Varanasi. Would this give him the answer, this most sacred of cities, the shrine of so many of the gods? As he made his way through the narrow streets, jostled by pilgrims, sight-seers and sacred cows, he was conscious of a heavy atmosphere, as if everyone had come with his load of sin and care and had left it there, and the weight of it all descended upon him and made it difficult for him to breathe. He watched the faces of the endless stream of worshippers as they went in and out of the thousands of temples. If they *had* left their load of sin and care there it seemed to make no difference to them. Most of them looked weary and hopeless. A few wore concentrated expressions of earnest devotion, but it was obvious that none had obtained what they were looking for.

Arjun went down to the sacred River Ganges and watched the worshippers bathing, drinking the water, offering prayers, flowers and coconuts to the great Mother Goddess. He noticed the same mechanical movements in the action of the worshippers as those in the Narbada River. Did they really care? Did it all mean nothing to them? He went up to one elderly man who seemed very devout in his ablutions. His face was saddened by a yearning expression which was the result of many years of performing the same exercises without finding his heart's desire.

'Have you found God?' asked Arjun, as the worshipper came up the steps from the river, drying himself with his *dhoti*.

The man gave a short, mirthless laugh. 'And how shall we find him?' he asked, looking at Arjun as if he ought to know better.

'Have you got peace now that you have bathed in the river?'

'Peace?' he asked in surprise. 'Where shall we find that?'

'Then why do you perform these acts of worship?'

The man shrugged his shoulders. 'What else can we do? It is the law of Manu.'

He passed on, mingling in the crowd of worshippers who were doing the same thing.

Arjun wended his way through the crowds along the riverside, and was turning towards the central temple area when he heard a sound that tore his heart—the slow, heavy rhythmic clash of cymbals and a drum beating: one—two—three, one—two—three. It accompanied the voices of women mournfully chanting the three chief names of Vishnu in unison: 'Krishna, Hari, Ram; Krishna, Hari, Ram.' It sounded like the heavy tread of weary souls, their voices crying out for light and truth.

Arjun went towards the sound which was coming from a temple near the river. He stopped in the doorway and gazed, awestruck, at the scene before him. About one hundred women clad in white saris, and wearing no jewellery, were seated on the floor, facing one another in rows. Some had cymbals, others clapped their hands in time to the rhythm.

As they chanted the names, some gazed around them with glassy eyes as they had lost the power to see with interest, and only a dull looking on as if they were something separated from the world. Others sat with head down, or looked straight in front of them in utter despair, mechanically repeating the names as if they were in a trance. Most were young women, some were even young girls. A few were older who showed resignation rather than despair on their faces. One of these, also in a white sari, came towards Arjun from the gloomy room.

'You cannot come in here,' she said in a toneless voice, glaring at him with eyes that had lost their soul long ago. 'This is the Temple of the Widows.'

Arjun retreated. He was horrified. His village widows were never treated like that. They certainly had to atone for the sin that killed their husbands, but they could at least stay at home and fast, and go to the temple to pray and offer sacrifices. But these poor Brahman women were doomed to live for the rest of their lives in such an atmosphere, being mesmerised by the deadening rhythm and monotony of the whole thing until many of them went out of their minds.

He made his way to the great golden temple in the heart of Varanasi. The bell was clanging constantly as the endless stream of worshippers let the god know they had come. They had brought bilva leaves and holy Ganges water to be placed on the linga stone by the priest. As Arjun entered into the dark abode of the god Shiva, he felt the same stifling sensation and atmosphere as he had experienced in Nagpur. He wanted to get out at once, but here was the god of regeneration, the Destroyer and Reproducer in his image of the black stone bull, the symbol of reproductive energy, and the linga, the symbol of the male generative organ, the life-giving force. Because god Shiva is always creating life out of death, his symbol is in a condition of perpetual heat and excitement, and requires to be cooled and appeased by the cooling leaves and water brought by his worshippers.

Arjun stood at the side of the square enclosure where the priest was busily applying the leaves and pouring on the water. Drums and cymbals were making the air throb. Here there seemed to be more earnestness in the worshippers, a superstitious fear and awe, with a seriousness which showed that for many this was a matter of life or death. Many had relatives who were sick or dying; some were childless women who were pleading for the creative life of the god to enter them and give them a son; others had feuds and grudges and wanted power to destroy their enemies. Arjun watched them all, his heart throbbing like the drums, conscious of that barrier of evil closing in on him, that invincible power which seemed to enter and proceed to destroy his soul without his being able to resist. He leaned heavily on his staff.

He did not know how long he waited, but eventually another priest came to relieve the one who had been performing the rites. As the latter turned to go, he saw Arjun standing there and paused. His forehead was marked with the three stripes of Shiva. His expression was lowering and forbidding. His eyes were piercing and shrewd as if he could discern the innermost thoughts of the heart.

Arjun put his hands together in salute. '*Namaste*, Swamiji. I have a question to ask,' he said faintly, his voice hardly heard above the din of the drums.

The priest continued to look penetratingly at him.

'I want to know how to find God.'

The hard look softened a little. 'Come to my room,' the priest said, and led the way to the back of the temple, across a courtyard around which were several small rooms. The priest unlocked the door of one of these and motioned Arjun to come in. There was no furniture. A mat was on the floor, upon which they sat. There was no window. The walls were piled high with books and papers. In an alcove in the wall was an idol of the goddess Kali, the wife of Shiva. The door was left open to allow light into the room.

'Where are you from?' the priest asked, looking at Arjun with interest.

'From near Nagpur,' replied Arjun. 'I have just graduated from the university.'

The priest smiled strangely. 'I was educated at Oxford in the U.K.,' he said. 'Strange that all the education of the West cannot satisfy us.'

Arjun lowered his eyes. 'My sister died when I returned home. It all seemed so futile then. I want to know where she has gone, and—where is God?'

The priest was silent for a while. Then he said, 'There aren't many people who come looking for God. They come to ask favours for themselves and others, but God himself...' He looked down and shut his mouth tight as if to suppress his emotion.

'Have you found God?' asked Arjun anxiously.

There was a long silence before the priest replied: 'We only find God as we are absorbed into his infinite essence as a drop of water is absorbed into the ocean. That comes after many incarnations for those who are not Brahmans. For us Brahmans there is only one more stage to go. We are God now. Some day we shall be greater than God.'

He rose suddenly and took a paper from one of the books by the wall.

'Take this,' he said, giving it to Arjun. 'Learn it by heart—the thousand names, titles and epithets of Vishnu. Tonight is new moon. Stand in the Ganges with the water up to your neck and repeat them there at midnight.'

Arjun looked doubtful. 'I have been told many things like this, but there is no truth in them.'

The priest smiled cynically. 'There are many frauds and hypocrites in the priesthood. But you have not stood in the Ganges before.'

'No.'

'Then go and see.'

'You are not mocking me?' asked Arjun incredulously, half doubting, half daring to believe that this at last might be the answer.

That cynical smile again passed over the hard face.

'No,' he said shortly and Arjun knew he was dismissed.

It was late afternoon when Arjun sat again on the steps leading down to the river and studied the thousand names and titles of Vishnu. He knew some of them from childhood, for he had heard his father repeat them every morning when he performed his devotions at the *tulsi* plant which stood in an earthen stand on their verandah. Others were quite unfamiliar to him and were used only by the devotees of Vishnu, the Preserver, the second person of the Hindu trinity. There was not much time to learn them, and he anxiously repeated them over and over again to make sure he would remember them when he stood in the water.

It grew dark. He had not eaten all day, and so eager had he been to get to the end of his quest that he had not felt hungry. It was meritorious to fast and he was used to going for long periods without food. He knew the busy worshippers were too absorbed in their devotions to offer him food, even if they had it with them. He walked slowly up and down the stone paving at the top of the steps, repeating the thousand names to himself. The crowds thinned. Gradually there was no one left by the river, no sound except from the clanging of distant temple bells and the drumming and chanting of devotees before their gods.

Arjun reckoned it must be almost midnight. He was about to descend the steps when the figure of a woman dressed in a white sari appeared out of the shadows of a temple wall near by. She put out her hand and touched him. He drew back.

'I'm not that sort of person,' he said sharply. 'And, anyway, I have no money.'

She sighed. 'You came to our temple today. We both have to earn our living—you have to beg in the day and I have to sell myself at night.'

Her voice sounded as if it might have come from a corpse. In spite of himself Arjun felt a strange compassion for her, where before he would have despised her.

'You have no means of livelihood?' he asked.

'We get starvation rations at the temple, the rest we have to get for ourselves after seven.'

'I'm sorry, I cannot help you,' said Arjun, descending the first step. 'I have to do *puja* in the river. I am looking for God.'

'God?' she asked, with a tension in her voice as if she wanted to scream. 'There is no God. Extinction is the best.'

Arjun was speechless. He felt he wanted to agree with her. He looked down at the inky blackness of the river.

'Yes,' she said, reading his thoughts, 'I have often wanted to throw myself in and end it all, like many of us have done, but—I'm afraid. I don't have the courage they had.'

'How long have you been here?' he asked.

'I was married when I was nine. A year later my husband died. I have been here ever since.'

Unable to give her the comfort she needed, Arjun turned from her and went down the steps. Once again he thought of Tara—she had been spared this also. Then if God was the evil, sensuous being he seemed to be in those temples, he could expect an innocent girl to receive that kind of treatment. But was he?

He paused at the water's edge. It was dark. There was not a glimmer of light except from a lamp at the top of the steps. The stars appeared spasmodically between the scudding clouds. A strong humid wind was blowing but it was not cold. He laid his staff and

bundle on the steps and went down into the water.
It was colder than he had expected. The snows were
melting in the Himalayas; and even though the
river had flowed for nearly a thousand miles
through the plains, it had not seen much sun during
the recent rains.

He waded in deeper and deeper until the water
reached his neck. The pressure of the current
nearly lifted him off his feet. The Ganges is always
a swift flowing river even in the dry season, but at
this time of year it was impossible to go out far without being swept away. Panting with the exertion of
trying to keep his balance against the current,
Arjun lifted his hands above his head as he knew he
should do while addressing a deity. He looked up at
the stars which kept disappearing and reappearing
behind the clouds. They seemed terribly far away—
as far away as God—looking down upon him,
seemingly indifferent to his desperate efforts and
unable to help even if they wanted to.

He began: 'O mighty Swami, Lord Vishnu, you
great Preserver of all men, hear my cry, my worship
of you, as I repeat your wonderful names which are
too many to number; but you have given us a few to
say in adoration of you...'

The pressure of the current against his body was
increasing. He had to lower his arms into the water
to act as paddles to keep his balance. This might
detract from the merit of his prayers, but he could
not help it.

He continued, 'You who came as the great Tor-
toise to churn the ocean, who brought up so many
treasures we had lost, including our Mother the

Cow; you who inhabit the sea as the holy Fish, the jungles as the great Boar; you who overcame the demon Narak, you Waikintnath, Narsinhawtar...'

He went on gasping the names. His body was becoming numb and he did not know how he could hold out any longer. With an uncanny horror he realised that this must be what the priest had meant when he seemed so sure he would find God here—one moment's relaxing of his taut muscles and he would be swept off his feet to eternity. Then came the battle: Why not let go? Why not join Tara? No one would know what had become of him. He would just disappear ... 'Wasudev, Ramchandra, Harishikesha, Narayan, Keshav...'

A great darkness came over him. He was in the river of the dead—the ashes of corpses disposed of at the burning ghats were thrown into the mighty Ganges, to be borne into heaven by the goddess; bodies of children who had died of smallpox were thrown into the river's depths; devout folk had been brought to die on its banks, with their feet in the river as a last hope to reach Nirvana. How many spirits were now streaming past him in this relentless pressure? It seemed as if all the hosts of demons were pulling at him to drag him under. His mind reeled, his voice grew fainter, he wanted to let go, he wanted to join Tara, but—'O God, help me!' he gasped.

A rope splashed in front of his face. 'Hold on tight,' said a voice from the steps.

Arjun made a great effort and grabbed the rope. He was hauled ashore. As he attempted to climb the steps he collapsed unconscious.

8
Swami Narayan

When Arjun regained consciousness he found himself lying at the top of the steps covered with his blanket. Dawn was breaking and already early worshippers were making their way down to the river to bathe. He tried to turn over, and groaned. His body was stiff and wet, and he felt cold and numb to the bone.

'How are you feeling?'

Arjun looked out from his blanket and saw a man of about forty sitting watching him. He was clothed in a white turban, white buttoned-up coat and trousers.

'Awful!' groaned Arjun, closing his eyes again.

'I'll get you some tea.' The man went off into the near-by temple and returned a few minutes later with a cup of tea.

'Drink this,' he said, sitting down by Arjun.

Arjun raised himself with difficulty and swallowed the comforting liquid.

'That's kind of you,' he said, putting the cup down. 'How did I get here?'

The man had been watching him with interest. 'The widow you were talking to came to call me. I am a watchman at the temple here,' he said. 'She likes you—says you're different from most of them. She had to go back to the temple at four o'clock so she could not wait. But she helped to carry you up the steps after we had hauled you ashore.'

Arjun looked down at the river, its muddy waters sliding smoothly by, giving little indication of the terrific force of the current. He dimly remembered the nightmare of his struggles.

'A minute later and I should have gone,' he said in awe. 'Do many worshippers survive this ordeal?'

The watchman shook his head. 'They couldn't end their lives in a better place—they get what they are looking for,' he said ironically.

'Then why didn't you let me go?' asked Arjun, rubbing his stiff limbs.

The watchman smiled whimsically. 'The widow wanted you.'

'But I'm nothing to her,' said Arjun crossly. 'I told her I had no money. And, anyway, I am leaving today—I cannot stay here, I—I'm going home,' he said on the spur of the moment. 'I'm not ungrateful,' he added apologetically. 'I don't think I really wanted to die. I—I was afraid. Please convey my thanks when you see her.'

'If you are so keen to find God, why not go to the *mahant* at Sarnath? Swami Narayan seems to know everything. Many pilgrims go there,' said the watchman, rising to go.

'Where shall I find him?' asked Arjun without interest.

'He lives in the grounds of the small white temple not far from the Buddhist *stupa*—anyone will show you. *Namaste!*' He saluted, picked up the cup and saucer and returned to the temple.

Arjun sat for a while, thinking about the events of the night. He was more moved than he cared to admit that that pathetic woman had been so concerned to save him. He wondered what her name was; what she looked like. Her face had been covered by her sari. He wished he could comfort her somehow. But how? He himself was needing comfort, chilled as he was, even to his very spirit.

He painfully stood up and shivered as the wind blew through his wet clothes. The sun was fitfully trying to shine between the clouds, so he wrapped himself in his blanket and put his robe out to dry on the steps. He sat watching the people in the river. None went into the water farther than his waist, and even then some had difficulty in standing. 'It was a wonder I stood it as long as I did,' Arjun thought. He felt so miserable in body and spirit that he wished he had drowned. But soon he was taking the road to Sarnath.

The *mahant* was seated cross-legged on a white cushioned platform in a small room which was bare, except for six oil lamps standing on brass pedestals at each side. Brahman priests were in attendance. Incense was burning before him, and garlands of flowers, money and food were placed before him by the worshippers who came seeking his advice, as if he were God himself. He wore white, and was bearded and corpulent. He smiled blandly at Arjun who placed his hands together and bowed.

'*Namaste*, Swamiji,' said Arjun weakly. He was feeling ill and had not eaten for two days. 'I am trying to find out how to know God.'

The bland smile did not alter.

'How can one know the Unknowable?' came the crushing answer.

Arjun stood gazing incredulously at him for some seconds, but that mask-like smile continued and the twinkling eyes had a hard glint. There was no further answer. Arjun bowed and withdrew. He picked up his staff and bundle, and sick at heart made his way back to the city. Now there was only one thing left to do. He would throw himself in the river tonight and that would be the end.

He started to shiver violently. A sharp pain in his chest made breathing difficult. Gasping and staggering he finally collapsed by the roadside.

'O God!' he moaned, 'let me die, let me die.'

9

Jungle Ablaze

Nine months had passed. Arjun was tramping through the hills of Central India to get back to his village home. He looked a very different figure from the proud well-dressed young man who had alighted from the bus nearly a year ago. His hair and beard had grown so long that none would have recognised him. He leaned heavily upon his stick as if bowed with age. There was hardly any flesh on his bones. Not only sickness, but discouragement and despair had aged him beyond his years.

It had been nothing less than a miracle that he survived that acute attack of pneumonia in Varanasi. It was a miracle in the first place that someone had cared enough to get him into the municipal hospital. A sadhu lying by the side of the road was nothing unusual, and if he was delirious it could probably be part of his devotions. But a policeman had recognised his plight and had him taken to hospital.

The young doctor had said to him a few weeks later, 'It is a miracle you are still here. Some power must be keeping you alive for a purpose.'

Those words made Arjun determine to continue his search in spite of his weakness, and as soon as he

was discharged from hospital he went on to
Allahabad, the junction of the sacred rivers Ganges
and Jumna. From there he continued searching far
into the Himalayas to the source of the Ganges,
meeting holy men, *mahants*, *rishis*, asking questions, questions, questions. But there was no reality
in their answers, none could say, 'Yes, I *know*
God.'

He even went into two Christian churches and listened to their services. In one was a dead formalism
which made it needless to ask any questions, for it
was obvious that they had not even tried to get to
know God. In the other was such idolatry that he
could not see any difference between that and Hinduism, and concluded that they must have found
Hinduism the better way and adapted their
techniques accordingly.

At last, utterly weary, and having lost all hope,
he turned his steps homeward. Having been to a
sacred spot on the River Tapti he was coming up the
jungle road from Harisal. It was full moon in the
month of May. He had rested from the heat during
the day. A Korku tribeswoman had given him a
good meal when he had passed through her village,
so now that the air was cooler he decided to go on
walking late into the night and rest again at noon
the following day. It was a steep climb up the hill.
He was breathing heavily when he came to a fork in
the road where a notice was pointing off to the
right. In the bright moonlight he could read,
Wairat. To the Deity.

He did not want to have anything more to do with
gods and goddesses, he was sick of anything that

called itself divine, but something compelled him to take that path through the jungle. He heard the whine of jackals and the short cough of a panther, but wild animals seemed nothing to him compared with the evil spirits he had been battling against all his long journey. He came out of the trees to a clear space with fields and pasture land. The path led up a steep incline to the top of a hill which is the highest point in the Satpur Range.

The freshly white-washed shrine of the goddess of Wairat gleamed in the moonlight. A strong wind was blowing from the west, the relentless hot season wind which covers the plains with dust and feels like a blast from a hot oven during the day. The tails of freshly sacrificed goats had been strung on a tree near by. Arjun could smell the stale blood and see the dark stain on a stone under the tree. The place was littered with broken coconut shells and lemon peel, the remains of offerings to the goddess.

Arjun peered into the shrine. The flame of an oil lamp was flickering violently in the breeze. By its light the staring eyes of the wooden idol glared at him with the same evil power that he had felt from the other idols. As he looked, the flame flickered out and left the shrine in darkness.

'Some goddess!' thought Arjun with a sneer. 'Can't even keep the wind from blowing her lamp out!'

He turned to go, but a red glow over the brow of the hill made him go and investigate.

Spread out below him on the hill opposite was the most terrible jungle fire he had ever seen. The whole hillside was ablaze. With the force of the wind the flames were leaping upwards hundreds of feet, and the tinder-dry wood and grass fed by the fire yard by yard until nothing could withstand the onslaught of that terrifying inferno. Arjun watched spellbound. What power and destruction!

Out of the roaring of the wind and of the fire a 'gentle whisper' spoke to him:

'The God who answers by fire, *he* is God.'

Arjun waited and listened. Was he mistaken? It did not come again. He knelt down and did obeisance to the fire. But—how could he get to know *that*? He would be destroyed in the attempt! Then he thought, 'The Parsees worship fire. There is a temple in Amraoti. I will go there.'

With his hopes revived once more and desire rekindled, he set off in good heart along the road that descended to the plains. His goal was in view!

10

The Enlightened One

Arjun crept into the small white temple that stood in tree-covered grounds outside Amraoti. There were no idols—nothing in the room except a white pillar on which a fire was burning in a golden brazier. He prostrated himself before the fire and waited. Was this really God?

'O God!' he whispered, not daring to look at the fire. 'Please, if you are the one I have been looking for, reveal yourself. Help me to know you. Answer my question.'

But no answer came. He waited a few minutes, then raised himself on his knees and looked at the fire. It seemed very small and insignificant compared with the forest fire he had seen two days ago. Was it really God?

Just then an old priest came in, carrying some charcoal in a copper bowl. He was clothed in a long white robe, and wore a golden turban. His beard was snow white. He was very old and very solemn. He emptied the charcoal into the fire and turned to Arjun. Arjun bowed and placed his hands together in salute.

'You are a Hindu?' The priest glanced at Arjun's saffron robe.

'I am looking for the true God,' said Arjun, rising to his feet. 'Can you tell me how I can know him?'

'There are four elements of Earth, Air, Fire and Water in which the Almighty has manifested himself and with which he created the world,' the priest recited in a mechanical voice from force of habit. 'Mother Earth brought you forth, the Eternal Spirit pervades the Air you breathe, Fire represents the mighty sun which destroys the evil and purifies the good, giving us light and heat, and Water brings life and nourishment. What more do we need? Worship them and you will be prepared for life in the hereafter.'

Arjun was disappointed. The words were so similar to others he had heard in his journeys. He looked at the fire.

'Where did that come from?' he asked.

The priest also looked at the fire to avoid Arjun's eyes.

'Er—that fire represents the Eternal Fire that burns in the sun and in the heart of the Earth, the source of energy and life.'

'Do you have to keep feeding it?' asked Arjun doggedly.

'I and my assistant keep it burning,' said the old priest, realising that here was someone who would not be put off with orthodox answers.

'I see,' said Arjun bitterly. 'It is just like any ordinary fire.'

'It *represents* the Eternal Fire,' said the priest weakly.

Arjun saluted and turned away, his hopes again shattered.

He wearily set out on the last stage of his journey. He would be home by tomorrow. He would forget about God, get a good job in the city, send Balkrishna to college, marry an educated wife, and build a nice house on the outskirts where his parents could live in their old age. His heart felt as heavy as lead. It had all been in vain. Why hadn't he let the Ganges sweep him away?

So absorbed was he in his own despairing thoughts that he did not hear the sound of a bullock cart coming behind him in the lane which he had taken as a short cut to his village.

'Would you like a lift?' asked a cheerful voice behind him.

He turned and saw the driver sitting between the bullocks. The man was about thirty years of age, wearing a simple shirt and *dhoti*, a *pagdi* covering his head for protection from the sun. He had a kind face. Arjun gratefully accepted the offer. It was late afternoon and in his misery he had been walking on, unconscious of the heat, and was exhausted. The cart noisily bumped over the stones and ruts, but village people are used to shouting.

'Where are you going?' yelled the driver.

'Talegaon.'

'That's near the Nagpur road, isn't it? Good! My village is half-way—Kurha. You can spend the night in my house and go on in the morning.'

Arjun was silent. It did not matter to him where he slept—nothing mattered now.

'Where have you come from?' asked the driver, with the usual art of the village folk in getting out one's life history in five minutes!

'Oh, everywhere!' sighed Arjun.

The driver turned and looked pityingly at him. 'You look tired.'

'Yes, I—I've wasted my time.' Arjun outlined his travels, his hopes and disappointments.

'You poor soul!' said the driver when he had heard it all. 'I found God five years ago!'

It was some seconds before Arjun realised what he had said. He clambered up beside him at the front of the cart.

'What did you say?' he asked, wide-eyed in astonishment.

The driver smiled. 'I said I found God five years ago.'

Arjun gripped his arm. 'Tell me! How? Who? Where? Who are you?'

The driver laughed. 'One question at a time! I am an ordinary village man, a Mahar by caste.'

Arjun instinctively let go of his arm. He had not touched an 'untouchable' before.

'My name is Santosh,' the driver went on unperturbed. 'I received that name at my baptism because "God is my delight", and I want to give him pleasure and delight too. And I know it is giving him pleasure when I tell you about him.'

Just then a *rengi*, a small two-seater bullock cart, came careering round the bend. The lane was too narrow for the carts to pass. Santosh reined up his bullocks and drew them as far into the bushes as he could. The *rengi* hardly slowed down, and as it passed it grated against the axle of Santosh's cart. Arjun knew enough of village life to expect a volley of curses and a battle of words from both sides, especially from Santosh as it was the *rengi's* fault.

'Oh, sorry!' said Santosh pleasantly. 'Hope no damage is done.'

The driver of the *rengi* glared at Santosh and drove on.

'It was their fault. Why did you apologise?' asked Arjun angrily.

Santosh smiled triumphantly. 'It is the privilege of Christians to be willing to take the blame!'

'You are a Christian?' asked Arjun in surprise.

'Yes, thank God! Five years ago my cousin came to see me from his village ten miles away. He looked so different that I asked what had happened. He said that he had been born again and he wanted me to be born again too! Then he told me about the Lord Jesus Christ who is God himself, who came especially to die as a sacrifice for the sin of the world—your sin and mine.'

Arjun looked puzzled. 'My sin?' he repeated. 'What's that got to do with it?'

'Leave that for the moment,' said Santosh understandingly. 'We don't usually realise what sinners we are until we realise how holy God is.' He looked at Arjun questioningly: 'Did you find a god in all your travels who was pure love, good and holy?'

Arjun laughed bitterly. 'There's not one! They are all evil, impure and vengeful.'

'Our God who came in the Lord Jesus Christ is the true and living God. He is utterly pure, utterly holy, there is none like him—and he *loves* us!'

Santosh spoke with such assurance which came from personal experience, that Arjun knew that here was the answer—from an outcaste! He had never heard anyone speak so before.

'The Lord Jesus shed his blood to purify us from sin,' Santosh went on, 'but he could not remain dead—he is the Creator, the Prince of Life. He rose from the dead three days later and he is alive for evermore, watching over us, preparing a place for us, and giving us his victorious life by his Spirit who lives within those of us who believe.'

Arjun listened hungrily. Here, within a few miles of his own village, was someone who could have introduced him to the True God, and he had wasted a whole year trying to find him in other places!

'But,' he spoke his thoughts, 'the Christians I have met don't speak like this. They don't seem to know much about their religion and they don't have the joy that you have.'

'No,' said Santosh sadly. 'Many people think that Christianity is another caste, that because they have been born into a Christian family they are Christians. But God has no grandchildren! To all who *received* him, to those who believed in his name, he gave the right to become children of God. You have to be born into God's family by the Holy Spirit to become a child of God. That's what it means to be born again.'

Arjun looked at him wonderingly. 'Is that why you didn't get angry just now?'

Santosh laughed. 'It wasn't much to get angry about, but as long as I let the Lord Jesus live his life in me, he reveals his victory over things like that. He has changed my whole nature.'

They were entering the village of Kurha. People who knew Santosh were looking surprised that he had a Hindu sadhu with him in the cart. 'You never can tell with Santosh!' they said to one another. 'He doesn't mind who he picks up as long as he can tell them about his God!'

The cart turned down a little lane leading to the outcaste section of the village. They drew up at a neat little mud house, the verandah of which was scrupulously clean. A pumpkin vine grew over the roof to keep the house cool and to give fruit in its season. A papaya tree loaded with fruit was growing at the back of the house where the waste water soaked into the ground.

The two men alighted.

'I have to put the bullocks away now,' said Santosh. 'My wife will look after you.' Then he suddenly challenged Arjun—'Have you ever heard of an employer trusting an outcaste with three hundred rupees?'

'No, never!' said Arjun emphatically.

'Well, I have just sold some grain for my employer, and I'm going to hand over the money to him now,' he touched the breast pocket of his shirt. '*That's* what the Lord Jesus does in a man!'

He led Arjun into the house, and Arjun was surprised at himself for the casual way he was able to enter the house of an outcaste. His Hindu instinct made him want to draw back from contamination. As a child he had played with outcaste boys, but had never entered their section of the village or their homes. That was taboo for a caste person. In spite of all his education, that instinct had remained. But this house was different. He did not feel contamination here, in fact he felt clean from its peaceful influence. The inside of the house was as clean as the outside, and bright picture texts were on the walls. There was no furniture. The string beds were kept outside in this hot weather as everyone slept in the open. A shelf of books was fixed in the mud wall.

'Bai!' called Santosh.

His wife came in through the door opposite from the cook house. She was a pleasant-faced woman and did not seem surprised that a sadhu, with long straggling hair and a beard, had come into her house. Her sari was old, but clean, and neatly mended where it had been torn.

'This is Krupabai, my wife,' said Santosh. 'She also received a new name at her baptism because the grace of God had saved her from sin and made her a new person in Christ Jesus. That is why she took the name Krupa (grace).'

'Bai,' he said, turning to his wife, 'this is—I'm sorry, I did not ask your name!' he said, turning to Arjun.

'Arjun Bhaskar.'

'He has wandered all over the north of India looking for God,' Santosh continued, 'and he is very tired. He is staying here for the night and will go on in the morning to his home in Talegaon. You will eat with us, won't you?' He turned to Arjun with a twinkle in his eye.

Arjun bowed respectfully to hide the reluctance in his face. Whatever would his people say if they knew he was eating with Mahars! But he could not refuse their kind invitation.

'I shall be glad to,' he said.

Santosh went off to his employer while Krupabai spread out a mat for Arjun to sit on. She gave him a glass of water followed by a cup of tea. Three of her four children stood looking at him curiously. The eldest boy, Yohan, aged nine, was out at play. Shanta, the eldest girl, was seven. She reminded Arjun so much of Tara, and again that longing came into his soul, but somehow it was now mingled with hope. Four-year-old David held his sister's hand ready to flee to his mother at the first untoward movement from the strange man. Surekha, the baby sister, was quite unperturbed, and crawled over to him to investigate. They were all clean and neatly dressed.

'You keep your family very clean,' said Arjun, who was used to living with half-naked, dirty village children.

Krupabai smiled proudly: 'The Lord Jesus makes us clean inside first, then we learn to keep clean on the outside,' she said.

'How does he make you clean?' asked Arjun, not having fully comprehended what he had heard from Santosh.

'By his precious blood,' replied Krupabai, relieving him of Surekha who was pulling at his beard. 'If we walk in the light, as he is in the light, we have fellowship with one another, and the blood of Jesus his Son, purifies us from all sin. That is written in our Bible, and I and many others have proved it true.'

Arjun looked at her in amazement. A village woman quoting the Scriptures! Why, even a city woman with average education would find it hard to remember all the intricacies of the Sanskrit writings of the *Vedas* and *Gitas*.

'Is the Bible written in Marathi?' he asked.

'Yes, it is written in many languages, but we have it in Marathi so that we can get to know God.' She took a Bible down from the shelf and handed it to him. He took it reverently.

'Do you know God?' he asked, already inured to expect the same ambiguous answer.

With absolute assurance she answered with a radiant smile, 'Yes!'

Santosh returned. While he was having a wash and Krupabai was cooking the evening meal, Arjun looked through the Bible and turned over the pages at random. He had never seen a whole Bible before. Extracts are quoted in the school text books, but many are misquoted, and the stories of the birth and crucifixion of Christ are told as fairy tales, and nothing whatever is written of the resurrection.

Santosh came in and sat down opposite Arjun who was sitting like a statue, his finger on a verse, his eyes glued to the place he had found. At last he looked up at Santosh, his eyes wide in wonder and awe.

'It—it says just what I heard that night!'

'What was that?' asked Santosh.

'The God who answers by fire, he is God!'

Santosh nodded slowly. 'Sometimes it is by fire, sometimes by a wind or earthquake, or just by a "gentle whisper" from his Word. He chooses different ways to speak to us.'

'The voice seemed to come out of the fire,' said Arjun. He told of his experience at Wairat.

'It is strange,' Santosh mused, 'but in my case also, God spoke to me by fire. A godly man was present at my baptism five years ago. He asked me if I would go to Chikalda with my family and learn how to read and write, and study the Bible and get better acquainted with the Lord and his people. I said I would go if I could find someone to look after my field and home while we were away. I had a field in those days, and we were able to support ourselves sufficiently with a few odd jobs thrown in. But God took care of the field! One night I was coming home late from market and I found my crops set on fire! It was harvest time. We were going to start cutting the following week—and there was our year's food supply going up in flames! It was because I had become a Christian. My relatives and neighbours had already beaten me and pulled the tiles off our roof. My wife had to suffer taunts and insults from the other women because she would not wear *kunku* on her forehead, and they accused her of living in sin with a man who could not be her husband. My children had mud and filth thrown at them. Shanta was nearly crushed by a bullock cart while she was playing in the road. The driver purposely drove faster to run her over, but thank God Krupa saw her in time and rescued her. In all this the peace of God was garrisoning my heart, and I was able to love my enemies as the Lord Jesus had told me to. But when I saw our food being destroyed, a terrible fear and resentment gripped me—I—I didn't know what to do...'

The remembrance of that awful moment made him choke, but after a while he went on: 'Then, somehow, that fire burned its way into my heart. I remembered that God had said that all our works will be tried by fire—whether we are holding on to ourselves and all we possess, or whether we abandon everything to him and live by his Spirit. Did I really want him to be my *all*? I heard myself saying, "Yes, Lord, anything, take anything and everything!" That fire loosed my bonds even as it loosed the bonds of some servants of God who were thrown into a fiery furnace many years ago. As I was being reduced to ashes, so the fire of his Love flooded my being and my heart was so full of joy. I raised my hands and praised and praised him in words I had never known before. It was *such* joy!' Tears came to his eyes as he spoke, his face radiating the joy of that fateful night. 'I had been baptised in water, but that night I knew what it was to be baptised with the Holy Spirit and fire, as the Lord Jesus had promised.'

They were silent for some minutes while Santosh wiped his eyes. Arjun looked at him with envy.

'That's what I want!' he said decisively.

Santosh smiled. 'It is God's will for you, but it is not easy. It's a hard road. The Lord Jesus warned us that if we are going to be his disciples and follow him, and really get to know him, we have to take up our cross daily. The cross is the symbol of death— passing the sentence of death on ourselves every day, ignoring, denying ourselves, so that his life can be seen clearly in us. If we are going to be witnesses to the fact that he is alive, we have to be witnesses also to the fact that we, our old sinful nature, have died! It isn't easy!'

Krupabai brought in the meal. The whole family

sat down to eat.

'You eat together?' asked Arjun in surprise. He had only known women to eat after their husbands had finished.

'Yes, of course,' replied Santosh. 'The Christian family is one unit in the Lord. Husband and wife are joined together as one body—she is my equal, only I have the responsibility of caring for the family just as the Lord Jesus cares for his people. We eat together to show our union in him. Let us give thanks.'

They placed their hands together and bowed their heads, the children following their parents' example. Arjun watched while Santosh prayed simply: 'Thank you, Lord Jesus, for this good food. Thank you for bringing Arjun to us. Help him to know you, and strengthen him after his long journey. Bless us together in your dear name. Amen.'

'You talk to him as if you know him—as if he is here!' Arjun remarked in awe.

'We *do* know him and he *is* here!' said Santosh, smiling in thankfulness for this assurance.

Arjun proceeded to eat the simple meal of bread and curried vegetables—home-grown vegetables from the garden, a thing unheard of at that time of year in the villages. He forgot his reluctance to take food in an outcaste's house. It seemed now that it was a privilege for him to eat with these people who could say with assurance that they knew the one whom they believed, and were becoming intimately acquainted with the Living God. The King was present at this banquet and he was an honoured guest.

'What is this place, Chikalda, of which you

spoke?' he asked, gratefully receiving another helping from Krupabai.

'You would have passed through it on your way from Wairat,' replied Santosh. 'What a pity you did not stop there. The school would be on now. We village folk who have just come to know Christ spend three months in the hot season and three months in the rainy season there. There is less work in the fields then, and those who have to live on daily wages can afford to be away at that time. The women learn to read and write like the men. That is why both of us can read now. Krupa can remember verses she learned by heart. She can also sew, and we all learned first aid and hygiene so that we can keep well. These vegetables you are eating are the result of what we learned—for we have fresh fruit and vegetables all the year round now by using the waste water from our bathing and washing. Our health has improved since then. The men do more detailed Bible study and we learn how wonderful is God's plan of salvation and how we can walk with him day by day. I have tried to go with my friends to as many villages as possible round here to tell them the Good News, but there are so many—that is why we have not reached your village yet.'

'Are there other Christians here?'

'Yes, ten families have come to know the Lord Jesus since I returned from Chikalda. I sold my field, because each time I planted grain people would turn in their cattle as soon as the young shoots were appearing and it would be eaten up. But these neighbours had been watching! The richest farmer in the village wanted a faithful steward and manager to see to his fields and stores. The very people who had persecuted me recommended me, for they saw how God had been with me. So now I have a good job, and these families come for teaching as often as they can. We have a service of worship on Sundays and we go out witnessing in the villages as many evenings as we can.'

'I must go to Chikalda,' said Arjun.

'But you are educated,' Santosh replied. 'You should go to the Bible Seminary at Pune. Many go there from all over India and many parts of Asia. All the teaching is in English.'

'I should like to,' said Arjun, feeling a little bit of the old pride returning at the acknowledged fact that he could speak English and was sufficiently educated to go to a place like Pune.

The meal was cleared away. Santosh opened his Bible and pointed out two verses in the book of Jeremiah.

'Here's a word for you,' he said, having discerned the trend of Arjun's thoughts.

Arjun read: 'This is what the Lord says: "Let not the wise man boast of his wisdom or the strong man boast of his strength or the rich man boast of his riches, but let him who boasts boast about this: that he understands and knows me."'

'Yes, I understand,' said Arjun, noting the warning, 'but education is useful.'

'Yes, indeed, it is useful; but it can be a snare!'

The men talked long into the night. At last they retired to their beds outside the house. Krupabai had already settled down to sleep with the children on the verandah.

11

Holy Fire

Once again Arjun was lying unable to sleep. He watched the waning moon shed her pale light over the sleeping village. The wind had dropped. The silence was broken only by the heavy breathing of sleeping villagers lying outside their houses, and the distant barking of a dog. The stars shone weakly in the moonlight. They seemed nearer and friendlier than they did on that—that terrible night...

'Lord—Lord Jesus!' Arjun whispered, his heart warming at the fact that he now knew whose name to call, that there was a personal God who was alive and who wanted him to know him. 'Help me to understand and to know you as you want me to, even—even though I might have to go through what Santosh has been through.'

He thought of those crops burning up—terrible when one has a family to support. Then he thought of the jungle fire. Santosh's words came back to him: 'We don't realise what sinners we are till we realise how holy God is.' How holy is God?

Arjun shut his eyes. He saw himself in the midst of those flames. Surrounded as it were by blazing purity and holiness, he saw himself in his utter littleness, his petty pride in his education, his rebellious will and total unworthiness—fit only to be burnt to ashes. He heard Santosh's voice saying, 'Our God is a consuming fire ... a refining fire ... His eyes are as a flame of fire...'

'Oh, my God!' Arjun cried out, 'then who can live in your sight?' He hid his face and sobbed, 'O Lord! Forgive me! I'm so wretched!'

Now he realised the hatefulness of sin. He remembered how he had wanted to dismiss God from his world and to live to please himself; and then how he had considered himself better than others because he was really looking for God, whereas they had only wanted favours. Pride! Self-pity! Self-righteousness! And then he remembered all the idolatry that he had committed from his childhood, and especially during the last year when he had so zealously worshipped many idols and not the living God. Memory after memory flashed upon his mind in the full light of him whose 'eyes are too pure to look on evil'. He was lost, hopeless...

Arjun felt a hand on his head. Santosh had awakened at his cry and was waiting for God's time to speak to him.

'Arjun,' he said quietly, 'if we confess our sins, God is faithful and just and will forgive us our sins and purify us from all unrighteousness.'

'But how can he?' sobbed Arjun. 'My sin is too great to be forgiven.'

'The blood of the Lord Jesus purifies us from *all* sin.'

Arjun was silent. Santosh prayed earnestly for him.

At last, heaving a great sigh of relief, Arjun grasped Santosh's hand and whispered: 'I've found him! Oh, I've found him! He—he's made me clean. I've got peace at last!'

12

Death to the Old Arjun

The next morning Arjun was sitting, washed and clean-shaven, looking more like his normal self, in Santosh's best shirt and *dhoti*.

As he sipped his tea, he said, 'I must be baptised!'

Santosh looked penetratingly at him. 'Do you know what baptism means?'

Arjun was not sure. 'Doesn't it mean publicly confessing the fact that I am a Christian, that I believe in the Lord Jesus Christ?'

'It is that—and much more,' replied Santosh. He rose and got a New Testament from the shelf. 'I would like to give this to you. It will help you until you can get a whole Bible. I will mark certain passages which you should read, and then we can see about your baptism.'

He placed pieces of paper between pages where he had marked certain verses, and gave the book to Arjun, who gratefully accepted it. He had made a request to stay with Santosh for a few days to learn more. Then he wanted to find a job to earn a little money to buy himself some ordinary clothes in the place of his saffron robe.

So after they had drunk their tea they went off to see Santosh's employer. On their way they passed a burly man with a scowling face.

'Out of my way, you son of a pig!' he roared, spitting on the ground towards Santosh.

'God bless you, Govind,' replied Santosh good-naturedly, and walked on.

'Did you hear what he said?' asked Arjun indignantly. 'He insulted you!'

'Yes,' smiled Santosh, 'but my Lord Jesus was spat upon and they slapped his face.'

'I—I'd like to slap that pig's face!' Arjun thought he was showing righteous indignation.

'Bless those who persecute you, pray for those who do spiteful things to you. When they were crucifying the Lord Jesus he said, "Father, forgive them, for they do not know what they are doing."'

'I couldn't!' replied Arjun. He was feeling that this Christian life was a bit too much!

Santosh looked at him and smiled mysteriously. 'No, you couldn't—not yet.'

They reached the farmer's house, entering it by a courtyard surrounded by a mud wall. The farmer's wife, daughter and daughter-in-law were sitting on the verandah sorting grain. Inside, the farmer was sitting on his string bed doing his accounts.

'*Namaste, Shetji* Saheb!' called Santosh cheerfully.

'*Namaste!*' Sakharam Satputi greeted him with half a smile. He was a thick-set, middle-aged man, wearing a Gandhi cap. He respected Santosh for his honesty and willing service, and although he would never admit it, he felt better when Santosh was around. Certainly he had prospered since he had started to employ him in his fields.

'This is my friend, Arjun Bhaskar,' said Santosh, introducing Arjun. 'He is needing a job for a few days until he can go to his village. There is little work in the fields now. I wondered if there was anything he could do for you in the way of book work.'

Sakharam looked at Arjun critically. 'Are you a Christian?' he demanded.

'I—er—yes,' Arjun stammered in embarrassment. He was amazed at himself. Last night and this morning he would gladly have told the whole world that he was a Christian, but in front of this hard-headed man of the world, and an orthodox Hindu, he was almost—almost afraid—ashamed? He felt Santosh's eyes on him.

'Can you do accounts?' Sakharam asked.

'I have not been trained in book-keeping, but I am good at maths.'

'I can give you half a day's work; I should only need you from nine to twelve. Can you stay now?'

Arjun said he could. Santosh went off to see to the hedging up of the fields, while Arjun settled down on the farmer's verandah with lists of grain sold and accounts due from people who were in debt to the rich man.

The morning passed quickly. Sakharam seemed pleased with his work and told him to come again the next morning. He would be paid at the end of the week. Arjun ate his midday meal alone. Santosh had had his early and was out supervising the work. Krupabai was outside making shevaya (a kind of vermicelli) and putting it out to dry in the sun.

Arjun took the New Testament and went down

to the Wardha River which flowed near the village. Despondently he sat down under a tree on the river bank. 'I'm a failure,' he thought, 'I've no courage, Lord. I thought I would have spoken joyfully of what you have done for me, but—why was it? Self-preservation? I let you down. Can you forgive me again? And then before that, my self-esteem or self-righteousness resented that remark made to Santosh. I was angry. I wanted to hit back. My self rose up—it's always my SELF! I'm not like Santosh. It didn't worry him at all. Lord, I want to be like Santosh!'

He began to read one of the places which Santosh had marked in the New Testament: 'Don't you know that all of us who were baptised into Christ Jesus were baptised into his death?'—So baptism means burial! Oh, no! Not that! Instinctively he wanted to preserve his life, to hold on to it, not lose it. He read on: 'We were therefore buried with him through baptism into death in order that, just as Christ was raised from the dead through the glory of the Father, we too may live a new life. If we have been united with him in his death, we will certainly also be united with him in his resurrection...' So there can be no resurrection without death? Of course not!

Arjun looked down at the water. A road forded the river at that point, and in spite of the hot season there was still a considerable amount of water. He watched a bullock cart go down the steep slope into the river. As the bullocks slowly waded in, he noticed for the first time that the yoke that went across their necks was in the form of a cross, the long beam passing between them. He remembered Santosh had quoted to him the invitation of the Lord Jesus. 'Come to me, all you who are weary and burdened, and I will give you rest. Take my yoke upon you and learn from me.' Did he mean, take my cross? Yes, the bullocks had gone down together into the water; they went up together out of the water on the other side. 'If we died together we will also live together!'

He read again: 'We know that our old self was crucified with him so that the body of sin might be rendered powerless, that we should no longer be slaves to sin.'

Arjun watched in awe as another bullock cart came down from the opposite bank. One bullock looked stronger than the other. When the weaker one stumbled, the strong one paused for him to recover, then pulled steadily on, taking the greater part of the load.

With trembling fingers Arjun turned the pages to another place marked by Santosh: 'I have been crucified with Christ and I no longer live, but Christ lives in me. The life I live in the body, I live by faith in the Son of God, who loved me and gave himself for me.'

Suddenly the revelation was given. The Lord Jesus had taken the old selfish, self-conscious Arjun to the cross with him and had put him to death. He was not fit to live! They had died together. And now? They were living together— the resurrection life of the Son of God!

Arjun kneeled down and committed his life to the Lord: 'Lord Jesus, I take your yoke, your cross, because just as that strong bullock helped the weak one, so you will help me. My self will be under the cross while you manifest your life in me. Oh, thank you, Lord, for showing me this. Thank you. Thank you!'

Joy flooded his soul. He had been put to death in the flesh and awakened in the spirit. The Truth had set him free!

He kneeled there for some time. Now he could understand why Santosh could ignore insults and take the blame cheerfully. A 'dead' man does not get angry and cannot feel insults! But he remembered Santosh's words, 'It isn't easy.' Even though the 'old self' is considered dead, there must be a daily assent of the will in co-operation with the will of God. No, he could see it was not going to be easy. But what joy to know that the Lord himself was taking the responsibility for his own life in him.

Hinduism, he thought, knows nothing of this. It says 'Know your self through much self-control and discipline, for in your inner self is the Eternal Self. That which is the subtle Essence in which all this has its existence, and that which is Existence itself—that thou art!' But how can man—who has raised his fist in rebellious defiance in the face of God saying, 'We don't want this man to be our king'—how can he get to know God by knowing himself? Man who is dead in transgressions and sins knows only the slavery of his sinful self; but death in Christ finishes him—he is set free from himself to do the will of God!

When Arjun got back to the house he gripped Santosh by the hand and said solemnly, 'I must go to my own funeral.'

Santosh's eyes gleamed with joy. 'So you understand?'

Arjun nodded. Santosh gave him a hug.

'Thank God!' he said, then added, 'But you must go home first and tell your relatives how much the Lord has done for you.'

13

Talegaon—and a Shock

The road entering Talegaon from Kurha passed by
Arjun's house. He came striding along, wearing a
new shirt and trousers which he had had made with
the wages he earned from the farmer. He kept his
blanket, water bottle and cooking pot ready to present to his parents as, after all, they did belong to
them.

When he entered the village he stopped dead.
The house he had lived in from childhood was a
ruin. The roof had gone. Charred timbers inside
showed that fire had devoured most of it. The mud
walls were broken down. It was a picture of desola-
tion.

'My—my family! Where are they?' he called anxiously to a neighbour passing by.

'They have gone to your mother's village,' he
said. 'This happened three months ago. If you had
been here you might have helped to prevent it.'

'What happened?'

A crowd was beginning to gather as the news got
round that Arjun was back.

'You know your father got into debt through
sending you to college, and last year's harvest was
bad. He had nothing to sell to pay the debt, so

Gopichand Wankhade took over his fields. But he wasn't satisfied with that and demanded his bullocks as well. When your father refused, Gopichand and his sons took the tiles off your roof and set fire to the house. Your family were out, but they lost everything.'

Arjun gazed at the ruin. So that had happened for his sake! How could he be reconciled to his parents now? He would tell them that he had found God—but at what cost—to them! And he had spurned the education and opportunity that they had sacrificed so much to give him. He glanced across to the alley by the side of the house and saw Atmaram, the eldest son of Gopichand, leaning against the wall leering at him.

'What price your B.A. now?' he mocked.

He was always a bully and Arjun had hated him in his school days. He felt anger and hate rising now. At the same time he felt the gentle pressure of the cross. It was a matter of choice—he could resist the pressure and let out at Atmaram all he felt, or he could accept the Spirit's restraint and co-operate in keeping himself on the cross. He again saw those bullocks crossing the river. He was going to stumble, but the Strong One held him up!

'B.A.?' he replied, with a calmness that was not his own. 'Why, it means more to me now than before. I am Born Again!'

With the joy of victory welling up in his heart he told the crowd what he had been doing and how he had found God, or rather, how God had found him. In all his journeys God had been following him, but the powers of darkness had been doing their utmost to keep him from seeking after Truth. Now they were going to do their utmost to get him down from the cross, and from his position of abiding in Christ. But they had failed this time.

Atmaram slunk away. The crowd listened, bewildered. This was not the same Arjun they had known.

'So you're a Christian!' remarked one of the men.

'Yes. I am identified with the Lord Jesus Christ.'

'What will your people say to that?' came the inevitable question.

'I don't know,' said Arjun sadly, looking at the ruin of his home. 'But becoming a Christian does not mean changing one's religion or caste in just the outward sense—it isn't some rite we perform to be called something different. It is being born again by the Spirit of God and becoming a new creation in Christ Jesus. It happens in here!' he said, pointing to his heart.

Just then his uncle came along. 'A fine way you've repaid your parents for all they've done for you! Going off and leaving them to face all this.' He angrily waved his arm towards the ruin.

'Yes, I'm sorry, Uncle,' said Arjun. 'I had no idea what was going on. But I have found what I was looking for, and I know God will look after us.'

'He's a Christian,' said someone in the crowd.

'A what?' shouted the uncle.

'I am a Christian,' said Arjun quietly. 'The Lord Jesus is my Saviour and God.'

'You mean you add insult to injury and break your caste, and pour contempt on your father's

ancestors by scorning their religion and … and …!'
His anger blazed. Jagnath was Arjun's father's
eldest brother and had as much influence in the
family as his own father. It no doubt was but a
reflection of what Vishram's anger would be when
he heard the news.

'And he didn't even get angry when he saw
Atmaram,' remarked the boy in the crowd.

'You have no heart for your old parents,' continued his uncle when he heard that. 'No
gratitude—you don't care what becomes of them or
their slaving for you.'

'Oh, my God!' Arjun groaned inwardly. 'This is
too much! If the grace of God is misunderstood,
how can I ever convince them?'

He turned away and went off in the direction of
his mother's village which was six miles away. He
would be there before dark.

14

Arjun Rejected

Arjun's thoughts were in a turmoil. Had he made a mistake? He had not honoured his father and mother as he ought to have done, yet the Holy Bible said, 'Anyone who loves his father or mother more than me is not worthy of me … Seek first his kingdom and his righteousness, and all these things will be given to you as well.' He had done that, but if it was all being misunderstood, what was the point? The joy and assurance he had known seemed to be crumbling away. He felt guilty, a worthless son. Satan, the 'accuser', was having his way with him.

The sun was low on the horizon when he was passing his maternal uncle's *mala*. His cousin Ragunath was unharnessing the bullocks after their weary hauling backwards and forwards, up and down the slope to the well, drawing up the leather bucket to irrigate the fields. Arjun was unaware of his presence, he was so lost in his miserable thoughts.

'Ho, Arjun!' cried Ragunath. 'You've come at last!'

Arjun paused and smiled wearily.

'Come and see my mangoes!' shouted Ragunath, leading his bullocks towards the gate.

Arjun went into the orchard. There were some

mango cuttings newly grafted in the old trees. Others had already grown into the foster tree and were ready to bear fruit next year.

'See how well they're taking,' said Ragunath proudly. 'They are a fine type of mango and should sell well.'

Arjun gazed at the grafts which had been bound in to the cut, or wound, of the tree with oiled cloth and tied round with strong cord. He remembered Santosh's words: 'You have been grafted into the death of Christ—that is the literal meaning of Romans 6:5. It is the same in 2 Corinthians 5:17, "If anyone is engrafted into Christ, he is a new creation". Keep remaining in his death. The devil can't touch you there, for while you are in that place you are covered with his precious blood. Just as the life of the tree flows into the branch as it lives vitally united to the tree, so his life flows into you, cleansing you and making you alive so that you bring forth his fruit!'

Arjun looked at the illustration before him and he quietly gave thanks. Peace reigned in his heart once more.

'There is something more than *rupees* there,' he said to Ragunath who had been waiting for a word of congratulation, 'something this world knows nothing about!'

'Where have you been all this time?' asked Ragunath, who was not interested in anything that was not of this world.

They walked towards the village, the two bullocks leading the way, one behind the other.

'I wanted to find out where Tara had gone, and I found God—the living God who made this world and who loves you, Ragu. He loves us all, and died to give us new life.'

'So, you found God!' said Ragunath with a sneer. 'And what good has it done you? You've lost your home and fields, and you have no job, have you?'

'Not yet,' said Arjun quietly. 'God will show me what to do.'

They approached Ragunath's house. Arjun's father was sitting dejectedly on the verandah. He looked up at Arjun without showing any sign of surprise or pleasure.

'So, you have come?' he remarked.

'Yes, *Bapaji*. I am sorry for what has happened.' Arjun sat down beside him while Ragunath went into the house.

'If you had got a job as I wanted you to, we would have been able to pay the debts,' Vishram said shortly.

Arjun was silent. What could he say? How could he quote verses which had been ringing in his ears, which he had memorised down by the river at Kurha and which he made his daily vow: 'Whatever was to my profit I now consider loss for the sake of Christ. What is more, I consider everything a loss compared to the surpassing greatness of Christ Jesus my Lord, for whose sake I have lost all things. I consider them rubbish, that I may gain Christ ... I want to know Christ and the power of his resurrection and the fellowship of sharing in his sufferings, become like him in his death ...' How could a man with his mind fixed only on this world's standards understand these truths?

It seemed now that God was going to take him at his word and divest him of everything, that he might reach his goal.

His mother was cooking the evening meal when Ragunath came in and told her the news, and she came rushing out on to the verandah.

'Arjun, my boy, my boy! You are home!'

He rose to meet her and embraced her. She started to weep.

'Why did you leave us? We didn't know where you were. If you had got a job we could have paid our debts.'

Arjun sighed. It sounded so much like the story of Lazarus' death he had read about in his New Testament—'Lord, if you had been here, my brother would not have died!' repeated by the two bereaved sisters in Bethany. 'Yet, Lord, you let Lazarus die,' Arjun prayed silently. 'You did it so that you could bring him to life again. What are you going to bring out of our lost fields and home?'

Drupadibai had to return to the cooking. Her old parents were still able to work, but she and her sister-in-law did the housework and cooking as the younger women of the family.

Ragunath came and sat on the verandah.

'He says he's found God,' he said, pointing his chin towards Arjun.

Vishram grunted. 'Lot of good that's done!'

'That's just what I said,' Ragunath said cheerfully. 'He wasn't even interested in my mangoes—

said there was something more important.'

'*Bapaji*, I'm happy about Tara now. I wanted to tell mother, but she is busy.' Arjun was praying desperately that he would say the right thing.

'So what!' retorted Vishram. 'That won't pay our debts.'

'But isn't it wonderful to know that she is happy and safe with the Lord Jesus?'

'With whom?' asked Vishram and Ragunath together.

'The Lord Jesus Christ has conquered death by paying the penalty of our sin, and rising from death —death is swallowed up in victory, and the Lord Jesus is alive for evermore. *He* has the keys of hell and death. Little children are safe in him through the merits of his blood. Their angels are always in the presence of their Father in heaven. Isn't it wonderful for Tara?' He was carried away with the joy and relief he had felt when he was first shown this truth.

'Who is Jesus Christ?' asked Vishram suspiciously.

'He's the Christians' God,' said Ragunath. 'We learnt about him in our book of religions at school.'

'Yes,' said Balkrishna who had joined them from his play and had greeted Arjun with a hug. 'I have a picture in my book. He had seven nails in his hands and nine in his feet.'

Vishram glared at Arjun. 'You're not telling me you have become a Christian?'

'Yes, *Bapaji*, I am born again by the Holy Spirit of God. The Lord Jesus has saved me by his blood. I am a new person in him,' Arjun spoke slowly.

'My ...!' shouted Vishram when he had reco-

vered from the shock. 'You throw over your education, you leave us for a year without any informa-
tion as to how you are or what you are doing, and
you leave your old parents to suffer when they can't
pay the debts they incurred for your sake, and to
crown it all—you become a—a Christian!'

Vishram's shouting had brought a crowd around
the house, including his father-in-law who stood in
the doorway glaring at Arjun.

'I don't want any Christians in my house,' said
the proud old *Kunbi*. 'You can get out of here if you
are going to persist in that nonsense!'

'But I must tell you the Good News,' said Arjun,
steeling himself for what might be coming.

'Good news? Good news?' shouted his grand-
father, grabbing a stick from a corner by the door.
'If that's what you call breaking your caste and
bringing dishonour on your father's name, you'd
better get out before I break every bone in your
body!'

'I am going to be baptised,' said Arjun, rising to go.

Vishram also rose and shook his fist in Arjun's
face.

'Cursed be the day you were born! That a son of
mine should bring disgrace on our family like this!
Get out! Get out!' His voice was shaking with emotion.

Several of the men rushed to get sticks, and
started beating Arjun while he descended from the
verandah. Others threw stones and dirt at him until
he struggled out of the village. Staggering along the
road a little way, bruised and bleeding, he collapsed
under a tree.

15

A Fool For God

The cool dawn breeze brought Arjun to consciousness. He painfully got into a sitting position, groaning as he moved his stiff limbs. His face was swollen and his hair was matted with blood where a stone had cut the scalp. Every muscle was sore and bruised. He thought of the time when he had been taken from the Ganges. At least he was not cold, and—there was a difference! This was for Christ's sake. This must be what is meant by the fellowship of his sufferings—the rejection of his love by others. He had certainly suffered the loss of all things now—his home, his family, everything except the clothes he was wearing, and even they had been torn. But he still had his precious New Testament in his trouser pocket. He pulled it out to read. His head was throbbing, but peace was in his heart.

'Blessed are you when people insult you, persecute you and falsely say all kinds of evil against you because of me. Rejoice and be glad, because great is your reward in heaven.' These were the Lord Jesus' own words.

'I can't say I'm joyful,' thought Arjun, holding his head in his hands. 'I'm aching all over, and—

Lord, I'm lonely.' He thought of Santosh. 'But then he has a family who shared his sufferings during that time. I am alone.' Then he remembered that the Lord had promised to give back more than we had ever left for his sake—parents, brothers, lands, as well as persecutions and eternal life!

'I wonder how you will fulfil your Word, Lord?' he prayed. 'You have certainly given me fathers, mothers, sisters and brothers in the little church in Kurha. They are dear people who have welcomed me, and they understand. But houses and lands? Well, they can wait. I will go back to Kurha now and be baptised.'

He struggled to his feet, stifling his groans, and started limping along the dusty road. The sun grew hot. There was little traffic along the road, for work was finished in the fields. The ground lay hard and dry waiting for the first rains. A cloth seller, carrying a bundle on his head, passed him and stared at him as if he had seen a ghost. 'I must be looking a mess,' thought Arjun as he looked down and noticed the blood stains on his shirt and hands. When he reached the road that turned off to his village, he went across the common to the lake and washed himself. The women doing the washing there stared at him. He knew some of them but they would not speak to him. The news of his becoming a Christian had spread like wildfire, and they were afraid to show any sign of recognition.

He went on. By midday he was utterly exhausted. He had had no food for two days and his wounds increased his thirst in the glazing heat of early June. He sank down under a babul tree and once more wished he could die. Then he was conscious of a cart slowing down.

'So this is what comes of being a Christian!'

Arjun opened his eyes. It was Gopichand with one of his sons, sneering at him.

'You fool!' they shouted as they drove on.

The devil hits a man when he is down. Arjun lay in despair. Yes, perhaps he was a fool. Just think what he could have been earning by now! His father's debts would have been paid, his parents might be living in a nice new house he had built for them. Balkrishna could have been going to the city high school, preparing for college. And what a worthless, disloyal son he had been to let his family down like this. This last blow would break his mother's heart—he would be responsible for her death. Yes, he was a fool, and worse than a fool—a murderer, a rebel ... He felt condemned by God, man and himself. He had forgotten 'the accuser' who was making the most of his opportunity. But Santosh had taught him well. He knew the pitfalls of a young Christian, and how despair and discouragement, as well as over-confidence and assurance, can get a man down and draw him out of his position in Christ.

The word 'fool' reminded Arjun of a passage Santosh had explained to him in Corinthians: 'God has put us apostles on display at the end of the procession, like men condemned to die in the arena. We have been made a spectacle to the whole universe, to angels as well as to men. We are fools for Christ ... We were under great pressure, far beyond our ability to endure, so that we despaired even of life. Indeed, in our hearts we felt the sentence of death. But this happened that we might not rely on ourselves but on God, who raises the dead.' And that was written by the Apostle Paul who said he had strength for all things through Christ who infused inner strength into him!

'God who raises the dead!' Arjun's heart leapt. He sat up. 'The power outflowing from his resurrection which it exerts over believers ... Christ who infuses inner strength into me.'

'Lord, how foolish I've been!' Arjun cried. 'I've been listening to the devil. Forgive me. I'm so slow to learn.'

Strength came into his body. His head no longer ached. His thirst had gone—he was drinking from the Fountain of Life. He still had to walk slowly, but received strength to get to Santosh's home in Kurha.

16

A New Man

Nearly the whole village of Kurha had gathered on the banks of the river to watch the baptism of a caste man. They had grown accustomed to the outcastes being baptised. No one took much notice of that—they had nothing to lose by becoming Christians, no prestige, not much money or property, and they might even better themselves by their contacts with Western missionaries who would get their children educated, and give them milk powder, and even clothes and money when necessary. But a *Kunbi*—that was different! He was not of their village. They knew nothing about him. He had no relatives there, so there was no opposition, only curiosity. What had he seen in this religion to make him want to change, to lose his home, and excite the opposition of his people and commit the 'unforgivable sin' of breaking castes—and, if that was not enough, to identify himself with the outcastes?

Pastor Thorat had come from Amraoti the previous evening. He also was a caste man and had suffered much for his faith. One of his front teeth was missing from the time when he was struck in the mouth for his testimony. He had been to Bible school, and was now not only pastor of a church

near Amraoti but also much used in preaching the
gospel. The previous evening a service of dedica-
tion had been held in Santosh's home. The Christians had gathered and had welcomed Arjun like a
long-lost brother. They had grown to know and
love him while he had been staying with Santosh.
Difference in caste and upbringing faded in the
bond of union in Christ.

The pastor had taken as his text Isaiah 43:2:
'When you pass through the waters, I will be with
you; and when you pass through the rivers, they will
not sweep over you. When you walk through the
fire, you will not be burned; the flames will not set
you ablaze.'

'The baptism of fire comes after the baptism in
water,' he said, looking at Arjun.

Arjun nodded and the pastor continued:

'The meaning of baptism is your testimony of
death unto sin, and a new birth unto righteousness.
If you have not died unto sin, then baptism has no
meaning for you. The power of his resurrection is a
life that is dead to sin and alive to God—"The death
he died, he died to sin once for all; but the life he
lives, he lives to God." His resurrection life, which
he has given you, is a life that has already died to
sin, and is alive to God.'

Now Arjun was standing by the river. He was not
feeling so elated as he thought he was going to be.
The Christians were standing around him praying
for him. Pastor Thorat was preaching the gospel to
the crowd and explaining the meaning of baptism.
But all eyes were upon Arjun. He was stripped to
the waist, and was soon going to be led down into

the water like a helpless child. How utterly
humiliating! The wonderful illustration of the bullocks had disappeared. He wanted to run away and
hide. The 'old' Arjun was making a violent death
struggle before he was buried out of the way for
ever! He had prepared a testimony he was going to
give before he was baptised, but the pastor had told
him that he was going to lower him into the water
like a corpse—and a corpse cannot speak! He felt
like a corpse then—a nobody—worse than an outcaste!

He felt the pastor grasp his hand and lead him
down into the water. They went in up to their waists
and the water closed over him.

Santosh waded into the water to receive Arjun as
he came out.

'Thank God!' Santosh whispered, as he threw a
towel over him. 'A new man in Christ has arisen!'

Arjun could not speak. He had met the Lord.

A hymn of praise was sung. The crowd began to
disperse, looking curiously at Arjun to see what
difference this had made to him, but his head was
lowered and the Christians were surrounding
him.

Sakharam Satputi, Santosh's employer, waited
until everyone had gone, then approached the little
group and spoke to Arjun.

'I would like you to come and do my accounts
again,' he said, trying to make it sound as if it was a
command and not a request.

Arjun looked at Santosh who whispered, 'He
likes your work.'

Arjun hesitated.

'I was intending to go to Nagpur to get a job,' he said. 'I have to pay my father's debts.'

'I will pay you a rupee an hour,' replied Sakharam, unwilling to humiliate himself further in front of these outcastes.

'Stay until after the rains,' said Santosh. 'You need more Christian fellowship for a while before you go out alone to face the world.'

Arjun looked surprised, 'But I'm not alone.'

Santosh gripped his hand. 'I know, but God has ordered it that we encourage one another while we can, and you still have much to learn.'

The rich farmer was looking on, mystified.

Finally, Arjun said, 'All right, if it is God's will I will stay till October.'

'Good,' said Sakharam, much relieved. 'Come tomorrow at nine.'

When he had gone Arjun asked in amazement, 'You mean to say he saw me being baptised?'

'Yes,' replied Santosh triumphantly. 'The whole village was there!'

'And he still wants me to work for him?'

'Among our people, where money matters are concerned, only a true Christian can be trusted— and I think he knows that, though he would not admit it!'

That evening a communion service was held in Santosh's home. Arjun took the bread reverently, awed by the revelation of the fact that from now on the Lord was his life. He had died, and his real life was hid with Christ in God.

'Your will be done in my body, Lord,' he prayed.

He took the wine, and by faith drank of the Spirit

who administers the cleansing, life-giving fountain.
He was joined to the Lord—by one Spirit.

17

Sakharam Counts the Cost

The days passed happily enough. In the morning Arjun would do the farmer's accounts and write some of his letters. In the afternoon he would read his New Testament and meditate. If it was raining he would sit on the verandah. If the weather was fine, he would go down to the river to the place where he was baptised, which was now a rushing torrent rising perilously near the top of the banks. In the evenings he could learn from Santosh who gave him the notes he had written when he was in Chikalda. Sometimes the Christians would gather and they would have Bible study together and share one another's experiences.

It was obvious that the Holy Spirit himself was teaching Arjun. His search after Truth had not been in vain, and to each question he had asked in his fruitless wanderings he found the answer in the Word of God. He was growing in grace and in the knowledge of the Lord Jesus Christ.

One morning Arjun was checking over the farmer's receipts with his account book and found that for one entry in the book no receipt had been given. Arjun looked up and asked Sakharam if there had been a mistake.

'No, there is no need for a receipt,' Sakharam said shortly.

'But shouldn't there be one?' asked Arjun innocently. 'There is such a lot of black marketeering these days, the Government are getting more particular.'

'That's none of your business,' snapped Sakharam.

Arjun immediately became suspicious. He remembered that Santosh had wondered why on some days Sakharam sent him to sell grain, but on other days he went himself, alone, not allowing anyone else to go with him—which was unusual for a farmer who committed most of his work to others. With his eyes opened to the possibility of what might be going on, Arjun found a lot of discrepancies in the accounts which had been done while he was away. What should he do? It was wrong for a Christian to have anything to do with the black market. Many poor people were starving because the grain they should have been able to buy at a controlled price was being sold at exorbitant prices in the black market. Yet he had no proof—only a suspicion.

He asked Santosh about it when he saw him.

'We'll ask God to show us what to do,' said Santosh. 'The grain I sell for him goes into the open market which is bought by Government agents who sell it at controlled prices. But where it goes when he takes it alone—who knows!'

That night rain was pouring in torrents. Arjun and Santosh were praying about this delicate matter when a messenger came from Sakharam.

'You are called,' he said. '*Shetji* is ill.'

'Both of us?'

The man nodded and dashed off.

The two men committed themselves and Sakharam to the Lord. Putting hoods of sacking over their heads, they went out into the rain.

'*We* have been given authority over all the power of the enemy,' shouted Santosh through the deluge.

'Yes,' replied Arjun grimly, 'but how to use it?'

They arrived at the house. The eldest son was waiting for them at the door.

'The doctor says he needs an operation, but the roads are blocked with the floods. We can't get him to hospital. He asked us to send for you.'

He led them into a room which was full of relatives and neighbours anxiously sitting round the bed, watching the agony of the farmer. Sakharam was rolling from side to side, moaning, and shouting at intervals. 'I'm dying! I'm dying!'

His wife sat on the bed massaging his stomach. The doctor stood watching them.

Thinking that the two men who had been called were some kind of medical men, he said, 'I think it is a perforated gastric ulcer. I have given morphia and streptopenicillin, but he must have an operation as soon as possible.'

'*Shetji*,' said Santosh, taking Sakharam's hand, 'you know the way of salvation. I have told you many times. But God wants you to confess your sins before he can heal you...'

The farmer's face was pale and drawn. Pain and fear were written on his features. He looked at the two men who had witnessed such a good confession for their Lord, who now stood calmly and sympathetically waiting to help him. Hope and confidence came to life within him. At the same time he was convicted of sin.

'Oh, my God, I'm a sinner!' he moaned. Another spasm of pain came on, and in fear he cried out. 'I confess my sins. I—I have abused my labourers—I have not paid them the right wages. I—O, yes, I—have sold my grain in the black market, I've cheated my fellow men. Oh, my God, have mercy on me!' he groaned, and hid his face in his arm.

Santosh leaned forward and spoke softly to him. 'God says he will forgive all your iniquities, and heal all your diseases because of the blood of the Lord Jesus Christ which he shed for you. Do you believe this?'

Writhing in agony Sakharam could not answer for some time. Then, breathing heavily and sweating profusely, he gasped. 'I—Oh, yes, I do believe—Oh, help me, God!'

Santosh turned to Arjun and said: 'The Lord Jesus said that we should lay our hands on the sick and they should recover. You place your hands on his head and pray.'

Arjun went to the head of the bed and laid his hands on Sakharam's head. Santosh placed his hands on his stomach.

To Arjun's amazement Santosh did not pray. Instead he commanded, 'In the name of the Lord Jesus, be healed!'

Arjun prayed desperately that the Lord would honour his name before the gathered company. He was afraid Santosh was not doing the right thing! Sakharam was screwed up in more pain than before. The people murmured in protest.

'In Jesus' name, and the power of the blood!' commanded Santosh.

With a sob of relief Sakharam relaxed and breathed freely. The people watched spellbound. Arjun continued in silent prayer.

'Oh, thank God, thank God!' Sakharam sighed.

Santosh prayed. 'Thank you, Lord Jesus. You have healed *Shetji*. Please now help him to receive your full salvation for his spirit, soul and body.'

There was dead silence in the room. The doctor felt Sakharam's pulse. It was beating normally. His skin was no longer cold and clammy, and his stomach and abdomen were relaxed.

'He's better!' the doctor whispered, awestruck.

Sakharam opened his eyes and held Santosh's hand.

'*Shetji*,' said Santosh gently, 'the Lord Jesus' warning to you is, "Sin no more lest a worse thing happen to you!" If you give place to the devil, he will take advantage of you in your body as well as in your soul.'

Sakharam looked at Arjun. 'You were right this morning. I should have given receipts for that money, but I sold the grain to the black market and I didn't want it known.'

'Have you repented, *Shetji*?' asked Santosh. 'Have you really turned your back on these sins, and do you promise to make reconciliation where you can?'

Sakharam was reluctant. 'Yes, I—I will do what I can.'

'Then God has forgiven you for Christ's sake. But he alone can keep you from doing the same thing again. Take him as your Saviour and Lord of your life.'

Sakharam hesitated. He was grateful, yes, but ... He sat and met the stares of his relatives and friends.

'He's better!' they murmured one to another. 'God must have done it!'

'Why did you send for us?' asked Santosh, while Sakharam was inwardly cowed by the strong bonds of caste.

'Because your God answers prayer.'

'And has he?'

'Yes.'

'Then?'

'Jesus Christ is God,' Sakharam announced to the company. 'I—I want you to worship him.'

'Him *only*?' queried Santosh.

Sakharam glanced at his family. His old mother was sitting hunched up by the wall, glaring at him threateningly. In the strange paradox of India the women are always the last to give way and to accept freedom from their bonds which have kept them as slaves for centuries. His wife was watching him anxiously, fearful of what the consequences might be. His elder son was looking sullen. He was to inherit the farm, and dreaded the stigma which would come on his family if his father decided to follow Christ. His daughter lowered her head. It was not for her to decide. His younger son was waiting expectantly. The whole company was holding its breath.

Finally Sakharam said, 'I am grateful to you, and to God, but I—I cannot become a Christian.'

His youngest son, Vijay, stepped forward. He was a fine boy of eighteen and was in his final year at high school.

'Father,' he said, respectfully, 'if you want us to become Christians I will gladly obey you. I have been watching Santosh and Arjun since they have been with us, and they are different. They have something that we don't have. And Arjun is a *Kunbi*—he is one of us! When he went down into the water that day I realised that it must have cost him something to go through that in front of us all. A man doesn't accept that kind of humiliation for nothing. Christ must be worth something, worth far more than we realise, for anyone like us to go through that!'

There was shocked silence for a few seconds and then the uproar began.

'The boy's mad! He's been bewitched!' the older men shouted.

'A son of mine will *never* become a Christian!' wailed his mother.

'You get right out of this house at once!' stormed the old grandmother, shaking her bony finger at him.

'Don't be such a fool!' said his elder brother coldly. 'You have your life before you. You'll ruin your opportunities.'

Sakharam sat silent. The cost was too great. He stifled his convictions for the sake of his earthly prestige and possessions. Vijay drew back, embarrassed and bewildered. Arjun was praying for him. He wanted to take him in his arms and shield him from the strife of tongues. How well he knew the confusion and turmoil that was going on in the boy's mind and heart!

Santosh raised his hands and shouted above the noise, 'What good is it for a man to gain the whole world, yet forfeit his soul? Or what can a man give in exchange for his soul? ... Salvation is found in no one else, for there is no other name (than Jesus) given to men by which we must be saved.'

The crowd became quiet again.

'But,' Sakharam looked in desperation at Santosh, 'can't I worship Christ *and* the other gods? After all, they are all the same.'

'Are they?' replied Santosh quickly. 'Would Arjun have been turned out of his family if they were all the same? Has any other god brought a salvation like the Lord Jesus?'

He turned to Arjun, grieved and angry. 'Come, we are wasting our time.'

The two Christians went out.

'What now?' asked Arjun, as they tramped through the mud to their home.

'We must be faithful in prayer. We must stand against the strategies and deceits of the devil, but it looks at present as if the fear of man and love of this world will hold him back. I have hope for Vijay though.'

'Yes, I had no idea his heart was so open. I have not seen much of him. He is eighteen. It is legal for him to change his religion.'

'And is that easy?'

Arjun laughed knowingly. 'No, it is *not*!'

18

Arjun's Opportunity

The rains were over. With his savings Arjun had bought some clothes to wear in the city. Instead of the showy zip bag he had at first, he purchased a cheap tin box in which to put his belongings. Gone were the cravings for the things of this world. All he needed now was food and clothing—and enough money to pay his father's debts and he would be content. His one aim in life was to please Christ, to know him, to become deeply and intimately acquainted with him.

Sakharam said nothing when Arjun took his leave. They had spoken very little since that fateful night. Arjun knew that he was paying his labourers the correct amount, and up to that time had not sold in the black market—but then, at that time of year there was little left to sell until the next harvest came round. There was little doubt that he was humbler and more pleasant to deal with, but he had shown no signs of daring the wrath of his family and becoming a Christian.

Arjun had met Vijay once on his way home from school. The boy looked round to see if anyone was watching, then he came up close and said, 'I do want to be a Christian, really I do, and one day I will, but—not now.'

He passed on before Arjun could answer and Arjun feared for him. Would he hold on through college when the things of the world loom so large and the opinion of one's fellows seems so important?

Arjun had hoped there might be some results from his short stay in Kurha, but, well—perhaps in due time. 'But surely there should be conviction from our testimony,' he thought, 'that heart repentance which cries out earnestly for salvation and a joyful acceptance of the Lord, no matter what the cost. Where is the power they had in New Testament days?'

'Lord, you have promised the power to be a witness, the power of the Holy Spirit upon us to convict unbelievers of sin, of righteousness and of judgement. I need that!' he prayed.

He said goodbye to the Christians and thanked them for their fellowship and kindness to him.

'You always have a home here,' said Santosh, giving him a farewell hug. 'But remember, God is your dwelling-place, your shield and very great reward.'

'I can never repay you for all you have done for me and been to me.' Arjun could hardly keep the tears from his eyes.

Krupabai pressed into his hand a lunch box full of good things to eat on the way. They saw him to the edge of the village and waved until he passed out of sight.

When he reached the fork in the road that branched off to his village of Talegaon he paused.

He could keep on to the left and reach the main road to Nagpur direct. If he turned to the right he would go through his village and reach the main road further on. But what was the use of going there? They did not understand, and what good could he do?

'Show them you have forgiven them,' said an inner voice.

'But I haven't forgiven them, at least, not really. I've tried to, but—anyway, what good would it do?'

'Show them!' said the voice again.

'But I have to go to Nagpur. I must get a job to be able to pay this debt.'

Then came the reminder of words he had read the previous day about 'the Holy Spirit who is given to those who obey him'. He did want the Spirit's power and fullness, yes, but … the struggle continued until finally he gave in and reluctantly turned up the road that led to his village. Atmaram and his wife Sitabai were working in what had been Vishram's fields. The crops were coming on well, and they were congratulating themselves on their unjust gain. They had left their year-old son asleep in the little hut of twigs and straw which they had erected to shelter them while they rested from the midday sun. Sitabai had been cooking and had left some wood still glowing in the mud hearth by the door of the hut. The baby awoke. He crawled towards the hearth, attracted by the pretty red glow. He picked up a piece of wood and waved it about, gurgling with delight as red hot cinders scattered around the walls. Then in his babyish way he started hitting at the wall. The straw caught fire and in no time the hut was ablaze.

At that very moment, Arjun was passing by. As the flames leaped out, he heard Sitabai scream, 'My baby! My baby!'

For a split second his old nature took him unawares, as the prospect of revenge seized his mind: 'God's judgement for them!' he thought.

But, like a flash, the answer came back: 'God's opportunity!'

Hardly knowing what he was doing, Arjun dropped his box, scrambled through the hedge and dashed into the blazing hut. Suddenly he was gripped by an overwhelming feeling of love. The child was screaming in terror. Arjun swept him up into his arms and backed out. His mother grabbed him and hugged him to her breast, weeping with relief.

Arjun was dazed. He sat down, trembling with shock and excitement. His hair had been singed and his clothes were scorched, but his skin felt nothing, only the scratches he received while getting through the thorny hedge. With awe and thanksgiving he remembered the promise he had been given at his baptism. 'When you walk through the fire, you will not be burned; the flames will not set you ablaze.' He had not been burned!

Suddenly he was aware that Atmaram was bowed on his knees before him, sobbing and utterly broken down. This was God's doing!

Arjun flung his arms around him saying, 'I forgive you, Atmaram, with all my heart I forgive you.'

Love poured through his being. Such joy welled up in his heart that he was laughing, weeping and praising God at the same time.

'How can you forgive me?' sobbed Atmaram. 'The way I've treated you and your family—I'm a cad—a devil—a——'

'Never mind!' said Arjun, keeping his arm around him. 'God is waiting to forgive you. He forgave me for Christ's sake, that is why I can forgive you. Now he wants you to confess your sins to him and take the Lord Jesus as your Saviour. He will cleanse your sin in his blood and give you new life.'

Trembling with conviction, Atmaram brokenly sobbed his confession to the Lord, pleading for his forgiveness and asking him to make him a new man like Arjun. Arjun could hardly believe his ears. This bully, whom he had hated from childhood, who had done what he could to torment him and his family—asking to be made like his enemy!

At last Atmaram calmed down.

'Has God forgiven you?' Arjun asked.

'I—I don't know. I don't deserve to be forgiven.'

'Do any of us deserve it? While we were still sinners Christ died for the ungodly, the righteous for the unrighteous to bring us to God. The blood of the Lord Jesus cleanses us from all sin.'

'Oh, thank you, Lord!' Atmaram murmured. 'I have a wonderful peace in my heart. Does that mean that he has forgiven me?'

'Yes,' said Arjun. 'Praise God! How gracious, how wonderful he is!'

Atmaram looked up and smiled. 'Yes, he is. If only I'd known it before I would not have treated you like this.'

'We can forget that now. God has forgotten

already. He says he has wiped out your sins as a thick cloud, and will remember them no more because of that perfect sacrifice of the Lord Jesus.'

'I must tell my father,' said Atmaram, rising to his feet. 'Come with me. We must give back what we have taken from you.'

He took his little son from Sitabai and kissed him. 'My son and heir! I nearly lost you, but God saved you—and not a mark on you!'

He carried him off to the field half a mile further on where his father was working. Arjun accompanied him, carrying his box, and Sitabai followed behind.

Gopichand was the most unpopular man in the village. He was a rich landowner and money-lender but was mean and miserly and loaned money at colossal interest. Anyone who had to fall into his clutches when money was needed for weddings or funerals or, as in Vishram's case, to educate his children, very seldom got out of debt during his own lifetime, and the accumulation of debt upon debt was a millstone around the necks of his children to the third and fourth generation.

Atmaram approached his father who was cutting a few unfruitful jwari stalks for his bullocks.

'*Bapaji!*' he called, 'something terrible was about to happen, but Arjun prevented disaster!'

Gopichand looked up puzzled. Atmaram told him what had happened, and then he added:

'Don't you think we should return their fields? And I will rebuild his house—a larger and better one, to repay him for his worthy act.'

Gopichand was impressed. He felt more amazement than he showed, that this man whose family he had so wronged was willing to risk his life to save his grandson. He looked from one to the other: at Arjun with his scorched clothes and the scratches on his face and hands; at his grandson, the first in the family and very precious. Of course it was right to return what he had taken by force and to let them pay the debt as they could. But—he would lose face in the village. It would mean admitting that he had been wrong, and it might start a rebellion against his crooked ways and would usurp the power he had over the people.

Seeing him hesitate and knowing his father well, Atmaram said, '*Bapaji*, if you are not willing to give back the fields, I will buy them from you and give them to Vishram myself.'

'And where will you get the money from?' his father sneered.

'I can earn it. I have fields of my own. It won't take long to sell the grain at harvest time.'

'Let it go,' Arjun intervened. He was embarrassed by this situation. 'I am on my way to Nagpur to get a job. As soon as I have saved enough money I can buy the fields back from you and pay any debt still owing.'

'I can't allow that,' said Atmaram emphatically. 'You have saved my son. You have brought me into salvation. How could I let this wrong we have done go unremedied?'

His father continued to look dubious. He had not understood Atmaram's reference to salvation. He thought merely of the Hindu concern that a son was needed to perform the rites necessary for the soul of the father to go through purgatory to the next incarnation.

Finally he turned away saying, 'All right. You buy the fields from me and do what you like with them.' He was not going to humiliate himself before Arjun by appearing grateful.

'Very well. Thank you, *Bapaji*,' Atmaram replied stiffly.

He and Arjun left the field and proceeded towards the village.

'I knew my father would not let them go without a struggle. But don't worry, you shall have them back by Holi Festival.'

'It will give you too much trouble,' said Arjun. 'Please let me earn enough to pay the debt. If you wish to build a house for my family, that will be sufficient. The rest I will see to.'

'No, no!' replied Atmaram. 'I must make amends for our sin. My father has wronged many people and I have co-operated with him. Now I must atone where I can.'

19

Atmaram Decides

When Gopichand returned from the fields that evening he found a crowd of men around his house. They were listening attentively to Atmaram as he gave his testimony and told what God, through Arjun, had done for him. Arjun was standing beside him. He was praying that God would break through the powers of darkness and unbelief and reveal himself to his own village folk. The *Patil* was among them. He was a stern, upright man who despised Gopichand, but had no authority to interfere with his underhanded ways.

As the crowd made room for Gopichand to go into the house, the *Patil* said, 'What has happened today should make you ashamed. God will requite your evil ways if you don't put things right. You should give back Vishram's fields and forget the debt. It would be merit in the sight of heaven.'

The crowd murmured its assent, but no one was very outspoken as most of them owed Gopichand something—at least until the harvest was in.

Gopichand, a coward at heart, glowered. 'I am giving them back when they have been paid for,' he said, as he disappeared into the house.

'I am buying them back from him with the profit

from my crops,' Atmaram explained to the men. 'In the meantime, I am going to rebuild his house.'

'We will help you!' said some of the men, and it was agreed that they would start work on it the next day as there was little work in the fields until the crops were ripe.

The crowd dispersed, but the *Patil* lingered until they had gone and then he approached Arjun. 'Your God must be very wonderful if he can wipe out hatred from your heart like that!'

'Yes, he is wonderful,' replied Arjun. 'And he alone could do it. The Lord Jesus died for people while they were hating him. When you think of it, we have been hating him all our lives because we want our will, not his. Yet he still loves us and forgives us. When we ask him to become our life, he gives us his love in our hearts so that we can love others as he does.'

The *Patil* gave him a long solemn look then turned away murmuring, 'It is wonderful, wonderful!'

Meanwhile Atmaram had gone in to ask his father if Arjun could stay the night there and eat with them.

'No, he can *not*,' came the reply.

'But father, what gratitude have you shown?'

Gopichand, who had been sitting disconsolately on the bed, rose and faced his son.

'And what gratitude have you shown to me?' he demanded. 'I heard you take the name of Christ when I came in. You've become a Christian like Arjun. You've disgraced your family as he has. You care nothing for your parents who have brought you up and laboured to feed you and give you an inheritance and position in the world. What gratitude is that? You can get out, both of you. Your precious son can stay here and grow up in your place. I'll see to it that he doesn't become a Christian!'

Atmaram stared at him incredulously. 'You mean ...?'

'Yes, I mean get out! I can't stop you working in your fields if you are determined to. You can pay for Vishram's fields when the grain is sold, but I won't have you in my house. You have taken sides against your father with his enemy. You are not worthy to be called a son of mine.'

'But—my son?'

'I said you can leave him. If my name is going to be carried on by him he is not going to become a Christian.'

Atmaram went over to the hammock cradle where the baby was sleeping. To have him saved from the fire and then to be parted from him in this way was too much.

'You can't part me from my son!' he said angrily.

'Then tell me you are not a Christian—and give up the idea of building that house.'

Atmaram gripped the rope that was holding the hammock and looked at his son. Arjun was standing in the doorway. His heart went out to him as the agony of decision brought the sweat to Atmaram's brow. This was God's battle against the forces of evil and must be won in the realm of the spirit. In the suspense Arjun silently claimed victory. 'Jesus *is* Victor!' he repeated deliberately as he withstood, in the spirit, the onslaughts of the enemy.

Atmaram turned abruptly and went out into the street. Arjun followed him. Neither of them spoke. They went to the ruins of Arjun's house and there poured out their hearts to God, and committed their lives and the lives of their families into his hands.

20

Arjun to the Rescue!

The next morning when the men who had volunteered to build the house arrived at the site, they were faced by a band of Gopichand's labourers, led by his four other sons, armed with sticks. Arjun and Atmaram had spent the night in the ruins and had gone off to wash in the lake. They had had nothing to eat for no one knew of their plight. When they returned a fierce argument was going on between the men.

'We should call the police,' said the men who had come to work.

'That won't do any good,' sneered Ganpat, one of the sons. 'My father's got enough money to keep them quiet! You can go away. He is *not* going to let this house be rebuilt.'

Arjun and Atmaram exchanged looks.

'Let it go please, friends,' said Arjun. 'It is good of you to want to help, but it will cause trouble. I will get a job and make things right with Gopichand.'

'Yeah! You can get out of this place altogether—both of you!' shouted Ganpat, raising his stick. 'My father doesn't want to see or hear any more of you.'

The people withdrew and the two outcastes went

to the *Patil*. When he heard what had happened he insisted that they should stay with him until something could be done. He was even more impressed that Atmaram had chosen Christ rather than his son, and determined to hear more about this wonderful God. Arjun stayed for a few days, teaching him and Atmaram from his New Testament. Then retrieving his box from Gopichand's house he set off once more for Nagpur—and once more the Lord seemed to prevent him!

That morning Gopichand was letting his buffaloes out from the small stockade in his field to graze on what was left of the dry grass on the common. He kept the male buffalo back to give it buttermilk, for it had a kind of dysentery. When it hesitated to take the liquid which was being poured into its throat through a bamboo tube, Gopichand still fuming from Atmaram's obstinacy, hit the creature harder than usual and it bolted off after the other buffaloes. To hold it back Gopichand twisted the rope, with which it was tied, around his hand and pulled with all his might, but the strength of the great beast was more than a match for him. He was pulled off his feet and dragged several yards over the rough ground with its thorny shrubs and sharp stones. When the buffalo caught up with the others, it stopped to graze. Gopichand was bleeding from head to foot, the skin torn off him, and his clothes were in shreds. He was so dazed and shocked he could not release his hand from the rope and lay in the hot sun, trembling, groaning and helpless.

As the sun grew hotter towards midday, his thirst grew unbearable. He could not move. His whole body burned and smarted. His arm remained caught in the rope which was kept taut by the buffalo moving slowly forward as it grazed. He wanted to shout for water, but no sound would come. His mouth and throat were parched. The throbbing and burning in his head and the blackness before his eyes were but a reflection of what was going on in his heart. Hallucinations and visions were passing before him as if he were in hell, deserted by everyone, desolate, hopeless, damned! He saw the village folk laughing at him in scorn. This was what he deserved! No one would miss him, no one would feel sorry for him. He was lost, destitute, and the world was glad!

In the midst of these tormenting dreams he felt his head being tenderly lifted, and a cool damp cloth gently wiped the blood and sweat from his face. A cup of cold water was placed to his lips. He drank greedily. What relief! He looked up and saw a face regarding him with compassion and concern. It was Arjun!

The realisation made Gopichand's heart melt within him. In his weak condition he wept like a child and clung to Arjun's hand.

'Let me get you into the shade and I will fetch a cart,' said Arjun, gently lifting him up and supporting his body. With Gopichand's arms around his neck he half carried and half dragged him to the shade of a tree. After giving him more water from his bottle and making him comfortable on some clothing from his box, Arjun returned to the village to find a cart.

'Thank you for your victory, Lord!' he prayed as

he went. 'I didn't want to help him. My old nature wanted to see him get his deserts, but you didn't let me have my deserts. You came down to where I was and lifted me up, and brought me into your presence with joy. Help me to do the same. Let this situation turn out to the praise of your glory.'

As Arjun came up to Gopichand's house he found Ganpat outside loudly boasting to two of his friends that he was going to come into Atmaram's inheritance. 'I shall be guardian to his son, and get whatever would come to him through his father,' he was saying.

He turned as Arjun approached. 'Get out of here!' he shouted.

'Your father has been badly hurt. We need a cart to bring him home,' explained Arjun.

'Who hurt him?' Ganpat demanded, grabbing Arjun roughly by the shirt. 'You did, I bet. You're making an excuse to cover up your dirty work. What did you do to him?' He stuck his face close to Arjun's.

Arjun felt the blood rising. He wanted to slap this insolent boy in the face. Subconsciously casting himself on the Lord for his control, he said quietly, 'The buffalo must have dragged him along the ground. The rope was twisted around his hand so that he could not get loose.'

'I don't believe it. *You* did something, you swine!' Ganpat raised his fist and struck Arjun a blow on the cheek.

Arjun reeled back, but brought himself under control. Gritting his teeth, he waited until the flash of anger had died down and then said, 'Hurry up, he needs you. We must get him home quick.'

'So you won't fight!' Ganpat leered. He turned to his friends, 'What do you think of that? These Christians are saps!'

The boys who had been watching Arjun's self-control with amazement had more sense than Ganpat.

'You'd better go and see what's wrong,' they said. 'We'll come with you.'

The bullocks were standing by the cart. They were quickly harnessed and the three boys drove off. Arjun walked on ahead of them.

When Arjun reached the tree where Gopichand was lying, he found him holding his right hand in agony. At the time Arjun released the rope he had not noticed that the circulation had been stopped through the continuous pressure. Now the hand was going gangrenous and the attempt of the blood to flow through the damaged tissues was causing terrible pain. Ganpat came and knelt down beside him.

'Baba, what did Arjun do to you?'

Gopichand held Arjun's arm with his left hand, and between his gasps of pain he said weakly: 'He's an angel of God—he saved my life!'

Ganpat avoided Arjun's eyes. He felt horribly guilty!

'Let's get him into the cart,' said Arjun.

They lifted him up and placed him on some straw which was kept for the bullocks' fodder on the bottom of the cart.

There was no doctor in Talegaon. Ganpat, trying to overcome his guilt by fussy officiousness, started to give orders.

'Tulsiram,' he said to one of the boys, 'go to Tivsa and get the doctor. Pandu, run on and tell mother to have some tea ready and hot water. Arjun, you sit in the cart by Dad and keep the sun off him.'

Arjun hid a smile. Another victory!

21

Recovery

By the time the doctor arrived, Arjun and Sitabai
had made Gopichand as comfortable as they could.
They washed him gently with warm water and
applied *halad* powder to the wounds. But the hand
was still painful.

Sitabai had secretly determined to bring up her
son as a Christian, as far as she knew how.
Atmaram's tremendous decision to follow Christ
rather than stay with his son made her realise that as
a loyal wife she must do the same, but she dare not
run away with her child until she had found a safe
place to go. She ignored the insults and taunts of the
family and neighbours when they mocked her for
being a deserted wife whose husband had broken
caste and was as good as dead, and she worse than
a widow—in utter disgrace. She had seen the love
of Christ during that incident in the field, and she
knew that her husband had done the right thing.
She was biding her time to follow suit.

The doctor examined Gopichand's hand.

'This must be amputated,' he said. 'You will have
to go to Amraoti for the operation. If you do not go
soon you will be dead within a week.'

'That is well,' said Gopichand meekly. 'I have

cheated and abused many people with this hand.
Let it be cut off!'

The doctor gave him morphia for the pain, and
wrote a note for them to the medical officer in
Amraoti.

As usual, the house was filling with people who
came more from curiosity than for sympathy for
such a man. The *Patil* was there and Gopichand's
sons—except Atmaram who was looking after
Vishram's crops. Arjun did not want a crowd
around him, but he felt constrained to expect a
miracle from the Lord. He sat on the bed and gently
took Gopichand's gangrenous hand in his.

'*Shetji*, do you believe in the Lord Jesus Christ?'
he asked.

Gopichand looked earnestly at Arjun and said
clearly, 'With all my heart I do. I have seen him,
and I am talking to him now!'

'I am but a representative of his, a child of God
by his grace,' said Arjun. 'I believe he wants to heal
you without that operation. It would be agony for
you to ride in a cart all that way, and very difficult
to get on a bus. The Lord has something better for
you.'

'I don't deserve to be healed. Let it be cut off,'
Gopichand said in resignation.

'We don't deserve any of God's good gifts, but he
lavishes them freely upon us and wants us to enjoy
them and to praise him, for *he* is our Life!'

Arjun spoke quietly. He was asking the Lord to
keep him sensitive to his will and to vindicate his
name in this godless family as well as in the whole
village. There was no doubt that Gopichand had

repented, but he needed that positive faith which would lay hold of all that God was waiting to give him.

'Did you hear about Sakharam Satputi in Kurha?' asked Arjun.

'Oh, yes. He was dying. One of the Christians healed him,' replied Gopichand.

'*God* healed him. I saw it with my own eyes. I was there. Now he wants to heal you!'

'You were there?' asked everyone at once. An atmosphere of expectancy had been created.

'Yes,' said Arjun. 'And what God did for him he can do for you in the name of the Lord Jesus who has conquered sin and death. Do you believe it?'

Gopichand looked steadily at Arjun. 'Yes, I do,' he said quietly.

Still holding Gopichand's hand, Arjun bowed his head and prayed: 'Lord, Jesus, you are the Prince of Life. Through your death on the cross you destroyed sin and took all the horrible results of sin in your body. Now you are alive for evermore, and have promised the gift of life to all who trust in you—by your wounds we are healed. Heal Gopichand's hand—show him that you are his Saviour from sin, and the giver of new life in the Spirit. You have shown your love for him, now show your power. We ask it in your name, and for your glory. Amen.'

There was an expectant silence in the room. Gopichand had closed his eyes.

'The pain has gone,' he whispered.

Arjun thought of the morphia. But then, Sakharam had had morphia and it did not deaden the pain completely. This must be the Lord's doing, and he would give him the glory. The *Patil*, who did not need many more signs to convince him of the truth of the gospel, came and took Gopichand's hand. He looked at it for a long time, then said, 'The colour is returning to normal!'

The people crowded around. Yes, it was! Gopichand looked at it in amazement.

'I can move it!' he exclaimed. 'It doesn't hurt. I can use it!'

Everyone gasped in wonder and awe. Ganpat with his three brothers drew back looking guilty and bewildered.

The *Patil* stood erect and announced to the company: 'I believe in the Lord Jesus Christ. He is the living God, the Saviour and healer of men. I wish to follow him!'

He faltered at the end as he realised the step he had taken before his people. But he remained firm. He had seen enough of the changed lives of Arjun and Atmaram to convince him that here was no mere foreign religion or philosophy of man, but the Truth itself—Reality. Being a seeker after Truth all his life, now, at last, in his old age he had found it!

The people stared and looked from one to the other. Gopichand was smiling happily and grasping Arjun's hand.

'I too will follow the Lord Jesus.' His face grew serious—'He has not only saved me from my sin, but he has revealed to me what I am! I can never repay him for all he has done for me, and I can never repay you for the trouble and sorrow I have caused you—and everyone.' He looked at the people.

'I gladly forgive you for myself,' said Arjun, 'but there is one request I would make—let Atmaram have his son!'

'He shall come and live with me again,' said Gopichand emphatically. 'He is my heir and he shall have my inheritance. You boys,' he continued, raising himself on his elbow and pointing towards his sons, 'you start building Vishram's house first thing tomorrow morning. It must be the best house in the village and completed in record time!'

Ganpat glared at Arjun, but said nothing. His father's word was law.

22

Reconciliation

While Vishram's house was being built, Arjun was guest of honour in Gopichand's home. He helped in the building where he could, and in the evenings he taught the Word of God to Gopichand's family and the *Patil*'s family. Others also slipped in unobtrusively and listened hungrily to the teaching. Atmaram had been received back with tears and apologies. It was a wonderful confirmation to him of what God could do for one who remained steadfast and faithful to the Lord, no matter what the cost.

Just before harvest time the house was completed. Arjun and Gopichand set out in Vishram's restored bullock cart to go to Pulgav to bring back the family. Vishram had just finished his morning meal when the cart arrived at the house. He stood on the verandah and gazed in hatred and apprehension at Gopichand, thinking that perhaps his son had made an alliance with him to wreak his vengeance and demand more spoil from him.

Gopichand alighted from the cart and took the dust off Vishram's feet, placing his fingers to his forehead.

'I have come to ask your forgiveness, and to bring you to your new house so that you may be home in time for harvest,' he said humbly.

Vishram was speechless. He looked question-ingly at Arjun, and his son smiled.

'It's true, father! They have built you a lovely house and have returned the fields, adding extra land as compensation for the trouble you've had ...'

'But—how—why ...?'

'God has shown me what a sinner I have been,' explained Gopichand. 'In his mercy he saved me, and your son has shown me how the Lord Jesus loves us and can change our lives. It is because I am a new man in Christ Jesus that I have come to make reconciliation and ask for forgiveness. There are many people in our village whom I have robbed by unjust usury. I am having to repay them as well. God has given me peace in my heart.'

Arjun could see the preconceived ideas and pre-judices that his father had against Christianity gradually breaking down, crumbling beneath the weight of this visible evidence of the power of a changed life. Still unable to speak to them, he motioned them to sit down and went in to tell his wife to bring tea.

When he rejoined them, Gopichand explained all that had happened and Arjun added a few of his experiences in Kurha.

When his mother brought the tea she looked long at Arjun, yearning to take him in her arms.

'My boy!' she said at last. 'Are you—are you still a Christian?'

'Yes, mother, I thank God I am!'

'It doesn't matter!' Vishram sounded as if he was coming out of a dream. 'It doesn't seem to matter any more!'

'Then we can call him our son again?' asked Drupadibai breathlessly.

'Yes,' mumbled Vishram.

Arjun rose to meet the embrace his mother was longing to give him.

It was not long before the entire village had gathered around and was listening to the astounding news. Gopichand's name was notorious in all the district, and his testimony confounded everybody. Drupadibai's proud old father had nothing to say. He would not give in so easily as Vishram had done, but he could say nothing against Arjun any more; in fact, he felt secretly proud of him.

At last the family moved off with what belongings they had collected while they had been in Pulgav. Balkrishna was the only one of the party who was not rejoicing. He had been indoctrinated with anti-Christian propaganda at school, and reacted with the enthusiasm of youth against anything that seemed unpatriotic and unworthy of the traditions of the new Bharat*. The fact of his brother becoming a Christian had made him feel a traitor, and he had to face taunts at school about the disgrace that had come to his family. And now he was going to live with him, and perhaps—ghastly thought!—perhaps his parents would become Christians too!

'*Wa, wa!*'exclaimed Vishram when the cart drew up at the new house. 'You have built us a palace!'

*or, *India.*

Gopichand proudly opened the door and showed them inside. There were four rooms instead of the usual two, and a wide verandah which had been wired in to provide an extra room when necessary. There was plenty of room at the side of the house to keep the bullocks and buffaloes during the rains. Vishram and Drupadibai were thrilled. And to think, that besides all this, they had their crops which were yielding well and extra land to cultivate. No more debts to pay!

'I am grateful!' Vishram murmured, utterly taken aback at this unexpected turn of events.

'You have no need to be grateful,' Gopichand replied. 'This will hardly repay the trouble and misery I have given you. If there is anything you need, please tell me, and I will do what I can to supply it.' He put his hand on Arjun's shoulder. 'And none of us will ever be able to repay Arjun for bringing us the Good News and *showing* us what it means!'

23

A Day of Victory

The lake at Talegaon was surrounded by a large crowd of people. Not only the inhabitants of Talegaon, but from the whole district those who had known the greedy, grasping Gopichand, came to see what had changed this man, and to witness the symbolism of the death of the old Gopichand and the rising to newness of life in Christ. He had chosen the name Prabhudas (servant of the Lord)—'For whereas I have lived only to serve myself, now I will serve the Lord and live for him,' he explained.

Once more Pastor Thorat was preaching the gospel to this record crowd. Santosh had come with a group of Christians and others from Kurha. He had been overjoyed to hear the news from Arjun that sixteen people were ready for baptism in his village. They included Gopichand and his family, the *Patil* and his family and Vishram and Drupadibai. Even Ganpat was identifying himself with the despised people of 'the man who was despised and rejected by men'. He had not been able to resist the tremendous impact of the changed lives of his father and brother, nor had he forgotten the self-control of Arjun that day. Finally, and not without a struggle, he had come to ask Arjun's forgiveness, and in conviction and repentance he received salvation.

Santosh threw his arms around Arjun. 'The dying of the grain of wheat is bearing much fruit!' he said joyfully.

'I am praying that they might have the same experience as I had when I went down into the water,' said Arjun.

'They may not,' Santosh replied carefully. 'God meets each one of us in different ways, according to our capacity to receive and willingness for himself alone. Don't limit the Lord to your experience. He will do many wonderful and unexpected things according to his infinite wisdom.'

Arjun had one sorrow. His gaze scanned the crowd and especially the group of schoolboys who had gathered on their return from school at five o'clock. Balkrishna was not there. He looked behind him. There standing back from the crowd was his young brother, scowling indignantly at his parents who were preparing to enter the water. Arjun went up to him and put his arm round his shoulders.

'Now is your chance, Balu. Come to Christ now!'

Balkrishna angrily shrugged himself free. 'I'm having nothing to do with you!' he snapped. 'I'm only living at home because I've got to live somewhere while I'm at school. After that, I'm going!'

'You want to see Tara again, don't you?' Arjun was surprised at his own words. Suddenly the boy flushed up and tears came to his eyes. He turned away.

Arjun returned to his parents and helped his mother into the water.

One by one the new Christians were identified with Christ in his death and resurrection. As the old *Patil* came out of the water his face was radiant with joy. He raised his hands above his head, shouting, 'Hallelujah! Hallelujah!'

Arjun smiled, 'Yes, Lord!' he prayed, 'You do meet people in different ways. I could no more have said "Hallelujah" than fly on the day I was baptised!'

He felt a tug at his shirt. He turned to see Balkrishna beside him, tears streaming down his face.

'Tara would have been here if she had been alive, wouldn't she? She'd have been baptised?' he asked shakily.

'Yes, I think she would. Her heart was very open. She would simply have received the Lord Jesus as her Saviour like a little child, which we all have to become if we are to enter the kingdom of heaven.'

'Will—will the Lord Jesus forgive me?' asked Balkrishna.

'Yes, he will if you ask him.'

The boy hung his head. 'I don't know how to,' he murmured.

'Just tell him everything, Balu. He understands. You have heard me talk to him many times.'

'But you know him.'

'He wants you to know him too.'

They prayed together where they were. Balkrishna smiled through his tears and wiped his face with the tail of his shirt.

Vishram was just returning from baptism.

'Father, Balu wants to be baptised,' said Arjun.

Vishram's eyes opened wide with joy. 'God bless you, my boy! Praise the Lord!' he shouted.

Balkrishna went forward.

Pastor Thorat asked no questions. He had seen out of the corner of his eye what had been going on and he could trust Arjun's judgement. But there was one question: 'You don't want to carry the name of a Hindu god, do you? What new name are you going to choose?'

Without hesitation Balkrishna replied, 'Anand! The Lord Jesus has given me such joy!'

'So, Anand, I baptise you in the name of the Father, and of the Son, and of the Holy Spirit. The old rebellious Balkrishna had died, and the new Anand has risen in Christ Jesus. May the joy of the Lord be your strength!' He lowered him into the water.

Anand was the last one to be baptised, and Pastor Thorat was following him out of the water when it seemed as though an electric shock went through the crowd. A man came hurriedly wading in towards the pastor.

'Please wait!' he shouted.

It was Sakharam Satputi! He had been standing unnoticed in the crowd. Now he had thrown all reserve and pride to the winds, and humbled himself before all his acquaintances by baring his head and coming down into the water.

'I can hold out no longer!' he said breathlessly. 'I must take Christ. I must be baptised. God has been following me from the day he healed me. I have had no peace. I have not been able to eat or sleep properly. And now he has even conquered Gopichand.

He must have my life—I must have his!'

Arjun and Santosh had come forward. They and the pastor were speechless with gratitude to God.

The pastor placed his hand on Sakharam's head. 'Are you willing for this *shendi* to go?' he asked, indicating the lock of hair that every faithful Hindu wears as a guarantee for reaching heaven.

'Yes, let it go! It is of no use. Jesus is my Saviour—I look to him for salvation.'

Arjun had a penknife in his pocket. He cut off the hair.

'Do you still want to be called the "intimate friend of Ram"?' asked the pastor.

'No, indeed! What has Ram done for me?'

He turned to Arjun and Santosh. 'I want to be faithful to the Lord like you two have been. What name shall I take?'

'Why not just Vishwas [Faith]?' replied Santosh. 'Then you can tell people about the one whom you trust.'

'Yes, my name is Vishwas. I no longer ...'

'*Bapaji*, I'm coming too!' yelled a young man who dashed into the water panting and sweating, but looking wonderfully happy. It was Vijay, his youngest son!

'I didn't know you were coming or I would have got a holiday from school,' he explained, 'but when I heard you were here I thought "now's my chance"! And here you are being baptised too!'

Vishwas threw his arms around him. 'God bless you, my son! Now we can confess him together.'

Arjun was thrilled. That very autumn Vijay would be starting in college, and now he would have an anchor to hold him faithful through the ups and downs of student life. Vijay did not need to change his name. It meant Victory!

24

New Beginnings

The harvest was safely gathered in . Arjun had been helping in the fields during the day and teaching the Christians at night. The little church was being established in faith and love, and their Hindu neighbours marvelled.

One evening in March, when the meal was ending, Arjun said to his father, 'It would be good if you and mother could go to Chikalda where Santosh went. You would learn to read and write, and learn more of the Bible, as well as hygiene and first aid. Mother would learn sewing, and you could learn carpentry and other useful trades. You could lead the church here when I have to go.'

His father nodded. 'I should like to. Santosh has told me about it. Anand could stay with Prabhudas's family while school is on. He could join us later, and they would look after the cattle for us while we are away. You would like to go, wouldn't you, Bai?'

Drupadibai was still feeling shy at her new role of a Christian wife, and being able to eat with the men!

She smiled. 'It would be wonderful, but I am too old to learn now.'

'No, no!' said Arjun, laughing. 'Santosh told me

that people as old as the *Patil* go there, and they learn well—that is, well enough for their age, and you are by no means as old as he.'

'Look how bright your sons are!' said Anand. 'You must take after them.' They laughed.

Arjun sobered and said 'Bapaji, I have a request to make. I won't go unless you give your permission. For days I have had a longing to retrace my steps on that journey I made and find the people whom I questioned. I want to tell them that I have found him for whom I had been searching, and share the hope and joy he has given me.'

'Go, my son, and God be with you,' said Vishram, without hesitation. 'What he tells you to do, do it. I know he leads you and he will prosper your journey.'

'Thank you, Bapaji,' said Arjun, much relieved. 'Eventually I hope to go to Nagpur and get a job, but so far the Lord has put other things in the way. It doesn't seem to be his will at present.'

'I don't think it matters if you don't get a job,' said Vishram, whose outlook had been completely revolutionised. 'If God wants you to be a pastor or evangelist, go ahead! He has given us enough to live on here. There are no more debts to pay, and we should even have enough to be able to send Anand to college.'

Arjun could hardly believe his ears. But God had wrought such miracles in the last few months that anything was possible.

Within a week it was arranged that Vishram and Drupadibai should go to Chikalda. The school was beginning at the end of that month so there was no time to lose in making preparations to leave.

Arjun set off once more on his journey. The Christians had bidden him farewell and had prayed for blessing on his venture. They wanted to lavish money and provisions on him in gratitude for all he had taught them, but he refused.

'God supplied my needs the last time I went, when I was still looking for him. How much more will he supply them now that I am his child!' he said confidently.

He felt he would be more acceptable if he retained the appearance of a sadhu, so he started to let his hair and beard grow again. But instead of saffron he wore a white robe, a symbol of the clean, new life in Christ. Memories flooded back as he stepped on to the main road that led to Nagpur. It was Wednesday. Baliram should be along with his lorry soon …

It was evening before Baliram's lorry came in sight. Arjun joyfully held up his hand. Baliram stopped. His mate was with him this time.

'Do you remember me?' asked Arjun.

'You are not the same sadhu I picked up nearly two years ago, are you?' Baliram was probing into his memory and looking at Arjun with a puzzled expression.

'Yes. You told me to let you know if I found God. I *have* found him. I want to tell you about him.'

'Jump in!' Baliram shouted gaily. 'Let him sit in the middle of us, Petras.'

Arjun climbed in and sat between the two men.

'Got a different rigout this time,' remarked Baliram.

'Yes, the saffron robe is a symbol of a seeker—always searching, but never finding. This white symbolises what we find in the Lord Jesus Christ—peace, purity and a new life.'

'So you're a Christian?' asked Baliram in surprise.

'Yes, he is the true God, the Living God. When I found him I found Life, and all my questions are answered in him.'

Arjun went on to tell of his experiences and how he had come to know and love the Lord Jesus. When he had finished the two men were silent.

Finally Petras said, 'Well, I have never heard anything like that before. You obviously know whom you believe. I wish I did.'

'He wants you to know him,' Arjun replied. 'He is looking for you long before you start looking for him. It is only ourselves and barriers of Satan that keep us from him.'

Baliram remained silent. For once his philosophy would not come to his aid. At last he said, 'The trouble is, if what you say is true, if God is real, then he is someone to be reckoned with, isn't he? I mean, one can't live one's life ignoring him, going one's own way, treating this world as if it is our world instead of his, considering him to be out-of-date and of no consequence. He—he ...' Baliram slowed the lorry down and drew up by the side of the road. 'He would have to have all there is of me—if you know what I mean.'

It was growing dark. On a distant hillside a line of fire glowed where the grass was being burned by the villagers.

'You see that fire over there?' said Arjun, pointing in that direction. 'It is destroying the old grass which is useless and clogging up the earth. When the rain comes, fresh green grass will appear and provide food for the cattle. God is like that fire. He comes as a refining fire to burn up the sinful dross from our lives. Then he comes with his healing, cleansing power, giving us his very life by the Holy Spirit—as we abide in him and obey him. Yes, you are right. He must first deal with your sin and have all there is of you to be able to do that.'

Baliram was again silent, thinking deeply, gazing at the fire which burned brighter as the night grew darker. Petras was also convicted. His careless living and apathy, while claiming to be a Christian, were abashed in the presence of this living flame sitting beside him.

Baliram said softly, 'I guess that's what I need—the refining fire of God—that he may have his way with me. When my wife died, just before I met you two years ago, the bottom seemed to fall out of my life. That's why I turned to Communism, but it didn't satisfy. Will you—can you introduce me to the Lord Jesus?' His voice broke as he turned to Arjun.

'Let's pray now,' said Arjun.

The three men bowed their heads reverently.

If *you* would like to know more about the God who answers by fire, you are invited to write to the publisher, using the address at the front of this book.

GLOSSARY

Baba: Familiar term for father, Dad.

Babul: kind of acacia tree.

Bai: polite term for woman.

Bapaji: term of respect for father.

Bhagat: mendicant or witch doctor (devotee of demons).

Bhagwat Gita: sacred book of the Hindus.

Bhajis: balls made of lentil mixture, fried in oil.

Chapati: flat bread.

Dhoti: loin-cloth worn by village men instead of trousers.

Halad: yellow turmeric powder.

Ji: term of respect added to the end of titles or names.

Kunka: red turmeric powder.

Mahant: saint.

Mala: orchard and market garden irrigated by wells.

Manu: unknown saint who wrote many laws for Hinduism.

Mantras: incantations.

Mela: religious festival and convocation.

Namaskar, *Namaste:* words of greeting, literally, 'I worship the god in you.'

Pagdi: rough turban worn by village men.
Pakka: real, good, durable.
Patil: head man of a village.
Puja: act of worship.
Rishi: saint or seer.
Sadhu: holy man.
Shetji: polite term for landowner or merchant.
Stupa: Buddhist monument or shrine.
Upanishads and *Vedas:* Hindu scriptures.
Yoga: practice of union with God.
Yogi: one who practises yoga.